Why the Science and Religion Dialogue Matters

Why the Science *and* Religion Dialogue Matters

Voices from the International Society for Science and Religion

Edited by Fraser Watts
and Kevin Dutton

Templeton Foundation Press
Philadelphia and London

Templeton Foundation Press
300 Conshohocken State Road, Suite 670
West Conshohocken, PA 19428
www.templetonpress.org

Templeton Foundation Press helps intellectual leaders and others learn about science research on aspects of realities, invisible and intangible. Spiritual realities include unlimited love, accelerating creativity, worship, and the benefits of purpose in persons and in the cosmos.

Designed and typeset by Gopa and Ted2, Inc.

Library of Congress Cataloging-in-Publication Data

Why the science and religion dialogue matters : voices from the International Society for Science and Religion / edited by Fraser Watts and Kevin Dutton.
p. cm.
Includes bibliographical references and index.
ISBN-13: 978-1-59947-103-7 (pbk. : alk. paper)
ISBN-10: 1-59947-103-5 (pbk. : alk. paper)
1. Religion and science—Congresses. I. Watts, Fraser N. II. Dutton, Kevin. III. International Society for Science and Religion.
BL241.W47 2006
201'.65—dc22

2006008574

Printed in the United States of America

06 07 08 09 10 11 10 9 8 7 6 5 4 3 2 1

Contents

Preface vii
Fraser Watts

Part 1: Why the Dialogue Matters

1. Why the Science and Religion Dialogue Matters 3
George F. R. Ellis

2. Does "Science and Religion" Matter? 27
John Polkinghorne

3. The Science and Religion Dialogue: Why It Matters 33
Holmes Rolston III

Part 2: The International Context

4. Science and Religion: Where Have We Come From and Where Are We Going? 41
John Polkinghorne

5. Science, Religion, and Culture 53
Fraser Watts

6. The State of the International Religion-Science Discussion Today 63
Philip Clayton

Part 3: Perspectives from World Faith Traditions

7. Judaism and Science: A Contemporary Appraisal 75
Carl Feit

8. Is the Science and Religion Discourse Relevant to Islam? 81
Munawar A. Anees

9. Science and Hinduism: Some Reflections 91
B. V. Subbarayappa

10. Science and Buddhism: At the Crossroads 101
Trinh Xuan Thuan

11. Asian Christianity: Toward a Trilogue of Humility: Sciences, Theologies, and Asian Religions 121
Heup Young Kim

Conclusion: Science, Religion, and the Future of Dialogue 135
Ronald Cole-Turner

Contributors 145

Index 149

Preface

THE DIALOGUE BETWEEN SCIENCE AND RELIGION, in its contemporary form, has been most vigorously pursued within the Christian West. However, the time has come for it to transcend that narrow cultural context. Each of the world faith traditions has its own relationship with science, and the science and religion dialogue would benefit, in every context, from a greater awareness of how it is pursued in other faith traditions. This book arises from work of the International Society for Science and Religion (ISSR), and reflects the commitment of the society to an international approach to the relationship between science and religion.

This book also reflects the conviction that the dialogue between science and religion is of wide social and cultural importance. In many countries, there has been a growing separation between science and religion, reflecting a fragmentation of society. The underlying conviction of most of the contributors to this book is that religion and science each proceed best when they're pursued in dialogue with the other, and also that our fragmented and divided world order would benefit more from a stronger dialogue between science and religion. Out of these convictions the present essays are presented. They reflect a commitment to pursuing the dialogue between science and religion in an international and multifaith context.

The book begins with a trio of chapters by three of the most distinguished figures in the current dialogue between science and research, and are based on talks given at a remarkably well-attended public session of ISSR in Boston in August 2004. The authors reflect different backgrounds. George Ellis, a South African and Quaker, works on models of complex systems. John Polkinghorne, a priest in the Church of England, is a former theoretical physicist. Holmes Rolston, a Presbyterian minister in the United States, is concerned with human biology and environmental ethics.

These three are followed by a set of papers that place the dialogue between science and religion in international context. First is a paper from John Polkinghorne, given as the inaugural presidential address of ISSR in Granada in 2002. Next I write on the international significance of both science and religion, originally a paper given to a meeting of the Third World Academy of Sciences held in Trieste on March 7, 2003. Third, Philip Clayton's chapter (originally published in the *Journal of Islam and Science*) describes an interreligious project in the field of science and religion and offers it as a model for future work in the field.

The third part of the book has contributions from members of different world faith traditions, each looking at their distinct relationship to science, including Carl Feit on Judaism, Munawar Anees on Islam, B. V. Subbarayappa on Hinduism, Trinh Thuan on Buddhism, and Heup Young Kim on Asian Christianity. (The dialogue between science and religion is very different for Asian than for Western Christians.) The first three of these contributions are also based on papers given to the meeting of ISSR in August 2004. The book concludes with a summation by Ronald Cole-Turner, incorporating a critical consideration of the field of biotechnology and the ethical issues that emerge from it.

Fraser Watts
Vice President, ISSR

Part I
Why the Dialogue Matters

I

Why the Science and Religion Dialogue Matters

GEORGE F. R. ELLIS

The Basic Themes

The science and religion dialogue[1] provides essential benefits from religion to science and from science to religion—provided we reinforce the open-minded, nonfundamentalist tendencies on both sides. That is what I explore here.

Tempering Religion

On the religious side, there is the issue of religious dogmatism and hubris: the tendency to claim absolute truth for fallible religious beliefs (they can't all be true!). The scientific approach can temper this tendency and—realizing that faith will always be the core of religion—can help religious understanding relate more coherently to the evidence that supports faith. Crucial is the issue of discernment. Science can help in the understanding of how to both evaluate evidence[2] and understand the multiple ways that a single reality can be represented and understood.[3] It can thereby also be a force for progress in interreligious dialogue.

A primary issue here is the tensions experienced by religion in the face of the sweep of understanding given us by modern science, which undermines the faith of many believers. The science and religion dialogue can help in developing mature religious understandings that will be robust in the face of modern scientific discoveries; indeed, this is its core project.

Tempering Science

On the scientific side, we also face dogmatism and hubris: in particular, a denial of the full depth of human nature in some of biology, the human sciences, and neuroscience. Thus, an equally important issue is tempering the extremist claims of some scientists about the scope and implications of science. At issue are, first, the way we understand ultimate reality in the light of modern cosmology and physics, which underlies the nature of our existence, and, second, the way we see the nature of humanity in the light of the progress of modern biology. These understandings play a key role in how we see ourselves and so understand the meaning in our lives. Crucial consequences follow for how we treat people medically, individually, and politically. There is thus a need for more humanist views to counter scientific fundamentalism. The science and religion debate can help here as a strong force on the side of humanity against dehumanizing views.[4]

Part of this need is realizing and respecting the boundaries of science: agreeing on what is and what is not within its domain. Its imperialistic tendencies need to be tempered with a realistic view of what science in fact can and cannot do.[5]

Fundamentalisms

The crucial battle is against all the fundamentalisms that deny the multifactorial nature of causality and existence that elevate some simplistic explanatory scheme (which the proponent happens to be expert in) over all other considerations without taking context into account. The science and religion dialogue can help fight dogmatism across the board by bringing broadly scientific criteria into the search for truth, but not by denying the breadth of human evidence and the need for faith and hope, as well as rationality. This dialogue can emphasize all the dimensions of humanity and the crucial role of value systems that cannot be derived from science alone. In this way it can promote a consilience of very different worldviews that are attempts to view important aspects of the same underlying reality, giving up the need to be right in favor of trying to see what is actually there as seen from different viewpoints—all the time keeping in mind the need for the testing of theories and realizing the dangers of self-delusion.

Applied Values

Also at issue is how applied science impacts lives; for example, in terms of biotechnology, issues such as cloning, values in environmental decisions, production of weapons, and so on. What is the nature of the values that will guide our decisions? There is a key need for ethical values that science per se cannot provide: they can only come from religious and philosophical positions and can fruitfully be explored by the science and religion dialogue in an interfaith context.

The Nature of Humanity

Overall, the science and religion debate can be important in emphasizing the full dimensions of humanity, and in particular the crucial role of value systems that cannot be derived from science alone. Thus, apart from its role in deepening the understanding of religious faiths in important ways, it can be an important integrative factor helping all humanity in the way we see ourselves and the universe in which we live, affecting our quality of life in a crucial way. It helps us be fully human.

Cosmology and the Nature of the Universe

The first major issue in the current science and religion debate is the nature of existence. Why is there a universe with the laws of physics and boundary conditions the way they are? This context provides the foundation for our being, as it shapes the environment in which we exist. Is it based purely in the blind laws of physics, or is there some element of intention or purpose underlying its nature?

The particular important issue arising here is the *anthropic question*.[6] The way life evolves depends on the universe. We can consider universes with all sorts of properties: bigger or smaller; hotter or colder; expanding faster or slower; with different laws of physics, different kinds of particles, different masses for particles; maybe with different laws of physics altogether. As a cosmologist, one imagines all these different universes and considers what they would be like. In most of them there would be no life at all.

What is clear is that life as we know it would not be possible if there were even very small changes to either physics or the expanding universe domain that we see around us.[7] Many aspects of physics, if they were different, would prevent any life at all from existing. There are all sorts of subtleties if the whole is to work, allowing complexity to emerge; for instance, the difference in mass between the proton and the neutron has to lie in a very narrow range, and the ratio of the electromagnetic to the gravitational force has to be very finely tuned. If you tinker with physics, you may not get any element heavier than hydrogen; or maybe if the initial conditions of the universe are wrong it doesn't last long enough, or it's always too hot, or it expands so rapidly that no stars form at all. So all sorts of things can go wrong if you are the creator trying to create a universe in which life exists. We are now realizing that the universe is a very extraordinary place, in the sense that it is fine-tuned so that life will exist. Because of its specific nature, our existence is more or less inevitable. Since its start, it was always waiting for us to come into being (as well as other intelligent beings elsewhere in the universe).

In particular, it has recently been established that the universe is not at present slowing down as we would have expected but rather its expansion is accelerating due to a cosmic force known as the "cosmological constant" or "quintessence." We do not know why this force is there, but we do know that if it were substantially bigger than it is there would be no galaxies, no planets, no life at all. The question is why it has the value it has, when fundamental physics suggests it should have been hugely larger, with no structure at all forming in the universe and hence no life existing.[8] There are three main ways of trying to explain it.

Chance

The first option is to invoke pure chance. Just by chance everything worked out right. This is not saying that what happened is likely; rather, it is just what happened, and there is nothing more to say. The position is logically tenable, if you like to live with extremely thin philosophies, but it has no explanatory power; it doesn't get you anywhere. So it is not an argument that is popular in many scientific or philosophical circles.

Design

The second option is the good old designer argument: the way the universe functions reveals intention, the work of some kind of transcendent power or force. Life exists because this fine tuning took place intentionally. In simple terms, God designed the universe and the laws of physics operational within it in such a way that it was inevitable that life would come into being. Physics has this extraordinary ability to underlie the spontaneous development of complexity because that was intended to be the case. This is the theistic view.[9]

The Multiverse

The third option is the idea of a multiverse, proposed on astrophysical grounds by Rees[10] and on fundamental physics grounds by Susskind,[11] who bases his argument on the "landscape" of possibilities of string theory (the currently popular theory attempting to unify gravity with quantum physics). They and many others propose that the universe domain we see around us is not the only one but that there is either a huge number of other completely separate universes with differing properties out there, or we live in one huge universe with many, many different expanding regions like the region we can see around us, each with different physical constants, rates of expansion, and so on. In most of these universes life will not occur because conditions will be wrong, but in a few of them it will just happen to work out all right. Although there is an incredibly small probability of a universe existing that will allow life, if there exists enough universe domains with a wide enough variety of properties, it becomes essentially inevitable that somewhere the right mix of circumstances will occur and life will come into being.

The problem with this explanation is that none of these other universes or expanding universe domains can be observed. They are beyond the part of the universe that we can see, so whatever is said about them can never be proven right or wrong. In many cases, there is no causal connection with them whatever, so there is not even the faintest possibility of checking their existence or their properties. The justification for their existence is then supposed to be that it is an inevitable outcome of the underlying physics. But this physics is not tested—indeed it is probably not even testable—and it is at present not well defined. Even the definition of multiverses is unclear; for example, the space of possibilities envisaged is not clear.[12] In my view, this is a metaphysical rather than a scientific proposal. The distinguishing feature of science is that you can test your proposals via experiment or observation, and there is no way of testing this hypothesis.

One can suggest that belief in the existence of a multiverse requires the same amount of faith as belief in a God who creates one universe.[13] Either option is possible; we cannot prove without doubt that either is correct.

Furthermore, if there were indeed a multiverse, that would not necessarily exclude a creator God. She could have decided to create many universes instead of one. These options are not, in fact, exclusive. The multiverse proposal is not actually a final explanation; it just pushes the final question back one stage further. The issue becomes, Why this multiverse rather than that? Why a multiverse that allows life rather than one that does not? The crucial question recurs. One can choose to accept the existence of a multiverse as a matter of faith, but that does not solve the ultimate issue of whether random chance or purpose underlies it all.

Science and the Nature of Humanity

The second major current science and religion issue is, What is the essential nature of humanity in the light of modern biology; in particular, molecular biology and neuroscience? Here there is real potential for conflict between science and religion: we come up against the fundamentalist views of reductionists who produce incredibly thin views of humanity. On the one side, we have sociologists and anthropologists who say that our nature is totally determined by culture, that nothing else matters; on the other side, evolutionary biologists say we are totally determined by evolutionary history and the resulting genes, that nothing else matters. But both these factions cannot be right. In fact, both these kinds of causation are significant, but in addition the environment in which we live matters, and we have the ability to shape ourselves to a degree, through our own conscious choices. Personal choice matters, too. To claim that any of these aspects has no influence is simply wrong, for they clearly all do; but some fundamentalists make this claim. A clear statement of how they have done so historically and the negative consequences of this stance are given in *The Blank Slate*.[14]

It is an extraordinary phenomenon: people from sociology, psychology, evolutionary theory, molecular biology, neuroscience, philosophy, and so on, making claims that humans are far less than they actually are. They do so with great authority and, if you disagree with them on humanistic or religious grounds, you are greeted with derision. This is a really important area. Some promote a relativist worldview on the basis of anthropological and sociological reasoning; but if that is a true understanding, it applies to their own arguments.[15] Some promote purely mechanistic understandings: we are learning more about the way that molecular processes underlie the functioning of each of us, particularly through DNA as the store of our genetic heritage and through neurons as the basis for our minds. We have been gaining a remarkable mechanistic understanding of the way that life works and the brain functions, which is extraordinarily successful. The problem arises when the claim is made that this is all there is: nothing else is relevant or has any reality.

Neobehaviorists and the Mind

The current area where this approach is vital is that of neuroscience. Not only is it one of the most serious potential points of tension between science and religion but between science and an understanding of the fullness of humanity, as well. There are philosophers, psychologists, and neuroscientists who tell us that consciousness is an epiphenomenon. The mind is said to be a machine that determines our thoughts and what we do by computational algorithms, so that what we think are conscious choices are not real. Religious behavior, for example, is simply a result of these processes and has no deeper meaning. This is a real threat from the scientific side. Let me quote from Merlin Donald's book *A Mind So Rare*:

> Hardliners, led by a vanguard of rather voluble philosophers, believe not merely that consciousness is limited, as experimentalists have been saying for years, but that it plays no significant role in human cognition. They believe that we think, speak, and remember entirely outside its influence. Moreover, the use of the term "consciousness" is viewed as pernicious because (note the theological undertones) it leads us into error. . . . They support the downgrading of consciousness to the status of an epiphenomenon . . . a secondary byproduct of the brain's activity, a superficial manifestation of mental activity that plays no role in cognition.[16]
>
> Dennett[17] is actually denying the biological reality of the self. Selves, he says, hence self-consciousness, are cultural inventions. . . . The initiation and execution of mental activity is always outside conscious control. . . . Consciousness is an illusion and we do not exist in any meaningful sense. . . . The prac-

> tical consequences of this deterministic crusade are terrible indeed. There is no sound biological or ideological basis for selfhood, willpower, freedom, or responsibility. The notion of the conscious life as a vacuum leaves us with an idea of the self that is arbitrary, relative, and much worse, totally empty because it is not really a conscious self, at least not in any important way.[18]

But this is not, in fact, what is implied by the science, which has a long way to go before it properly understands the brain, and which has made virtually no progress at all in understanding the hard problem of consciousness (many of the hardliners, however, even deny there is such a problem). *A Mind So Rare* covers very well from a philosophical view the question of the mind and the reality of our mental efforts and choices. I find Merlin Donald's writings on these topics convincing. And, personally, I prefer to run this whole argument the other way around, starting with our daily experience.

Consciousness and conscious decisions are obviously real, because they are the primary experiences we have in our lives. They are the basis from which all else—including science—proceeds. It is ridiculous to give up that primary experience on the basis of a fundamentalist theory that ignores this fundamental data. And that theory is not even self-consistent, because if Professor Dennett's mind in fact works that way, then you have no reason whatever to believe his theories—for they are then not the result of rational cogitation by a conscious and critical mind. If his claims were indeed correct, then the entire scientific enterprise would not make sense. It is important to reiterate here that despite the enormous amount that scientists know about neuroscience and the neural correlates of consciousness, the different brain areas involved, and so on, we have no idea of how to solve the hard problem of consciousness. There is not even a beginning of an approach. So as to the causal efficacy of consciousness, I take it as a given that underlies our ability to carry out science and to entertain philosophical and metaphysical questions.

Influences on Brain Development

A main factor shaping the brain is its interactions with the external environment, embodying social, cultural, and physical aspects. This has to be the case for a simple reason: from the human genome project we have now determined that there are fewer than forty thousand genes in the entire genome. From these, we have to construct the entire human body. But there are 10^{11} neurons in the brain, each of which has up to one hundred, maybe even one thousand connections. That is 10^{14} connections. Hence the genome does not contain a fraction of the information necessary to structure the brain in detail, even if each gene is read many times. What the genome does is set up general principles of structuring the brain and broad functional areas, together with the senses, instinct, and basic emotional functions. All the detailed structuring of the higher brain is governed by the interactions we have with our peers, caregivers, the social and natural environment, and with our own minds, this development being shaped and guided by the genetically determined primary emotional systems.[19] So the genetic influence is very important in setting the basic structure, but all the detailed structuring of each of our brains comes through the combination of all these interactions. The social and cultural environment in which we live, together with the conscious choices we make, shapes our brains by developing the initial structuring provided for us by our genetic heritage. We are not helpless prisoners either of that heritage or of our underlying neural mechanisms, nor indeed of unconscious wishes. They all influence us in important ways, but do not undermine our own personal choices and responsibility.

This whole area of genetics and of what makes human identity is becoming more and more important as we get increasing control over the human gene, on the one hand, and grow in our understanding of the brain, on the other. The true ethical crunch is going to come as we increase our ability to interfere with the brain genetically. The kind of problems that face us through our increasing ability to alter how we are, are going to become more serious than ever. If you behave a little differently from everybody else, should you be corrected by altering your brain by use of the latest technology?

Physics and Determinism

Underlying humanity is the basic physical hierarchical structure: quarks make up protons and neutrons, which with electrons make up atoms; atoms together make molecules; enough molecules together make biomolecules; if you string these together you eventually get cells; cells make tissues, tissues make systems, systems make the organism, and organisms make communities. This physical structure underlies our existence and functioning. The issue is that some scientists, therefore, say that ultimately we are just machines: conscious choice is an illusion, with our minds just dancing algorithmically according to the Maxwell and Dirac equations that determine what happens. Life is a meaningless dance resulting from the mechanistic interaction of electrons and protons. The conclusion is the same as in the last section, but arrived at from a different stance: there it was supposed to be a consequence of the specific neural mechanisms that underlie brain function; here it is supposed to result from the physics, irrespective of the nature of neural functioning.

Top-Down Causation

A common view is that the only causal effect present in thc hierarchy of complexity is bottom-up causation: the attraction between tiny electrons and protons at the bottom causing everything else all the way up. In a certain sense, that is obviously true. You are able to think because electrons are attracting protons in your neurons. Yet, as well as the bottom-up action, there is top-down action: in the hierarchy of structure, the top levels are able to influence what happens at the lower levels. This action is what enables the higher levels of the hierarchy to be causally effective, and it occurs around us all the time. It happens, for example, in the physics of the very early universe, in the way that genes are influenced by the environment through the process of evolution, in the way that genes are read on the basis of positional information in the developing body, and it happens in the way that the mind influences what happens in our bodies.[20]

A key point here is the issue of human volition: the fact that when I move my arm, it moves because I have "told it" to do so. In other words, my brain is able to coordinate the action of millions of electrons and protons in such a way that makes the arm move in the way I want it to move. This chapter and the computer on which it was composed were created by human volition, clearly demonstrating that our minds are causally effective in the world around us. The goals that we have shape what we do and hence change the situation in the world as we act on it—for example, when building a house or making a cup of tea. This causal efficacy enables us to carry out actions embodying our intentions, which in turn is crucial to our existence as ethically responsible beings.

Information is causally effective, even though it is not a physical quantity but rather has an abstract nature that embodies purpose.[21] Because of this effectiveness it costs money to acquire information; it has an economic value. Social constructions, too, are causally effective. A classic example is the laws of chess. Imagine someone coming from Mars and watching chess pieces moving. It is a very puzzling situation. Some pieces can only move in one way and other pieces can only move another way, so you imagine the Martian turning the board upside down or examining the rook, searching for a mechanism that causes these differences; failing to find one, he invents a force field that acts on knights and a different one for bishops. But all this is in vain; it is an abstraction, a social agreement, that allows the chess piece to move only in these ways. Such an agreement, reached by social convention over many hundreds of years, is not the same as any individual's brain state. It is an abstraction that exists independent of any single mind, and can be represented in many different ways. It is causally effective through the actions of individual minds, but none of them by themselves created that abstraction or embody it in its entirety. It will survive even when they die.

Many other social constructions—including language, mathematics, science, and the money system—are equally causally effective. This already is enough to undermine any simplistic materialistic views of the world, because these causal abstractions do not have a place in the materialist view of how things function. Indeed, materialism itself is a theory, but a theory is not a physical thing. Its very existence denies its own fundamental premise.

Effectiveness of Ethics

Ethics, too, is causally effective. It is the highest level of the goals we have, because ethics is the choice of which other goals are acceptable. When you have chosen your ethical values, this value system then governs which goals are inside your acceptable boundary and which are outside. So this choice is, again, causally effective. For example, if your country believes that the death penalty is acceptable, the realization of that belief will be in the physical existence of an electric chair or some equivalent in your jails. If your country does not believe in the death penalty, they will not be there. Again, nuclear weapons are devastatingly effective in the real world in causal terms; the fact that they are constructed is the result of the values of society and consequent goal choices.

The embarrassing thing is that this causal effectiveness of ethics is obvious to the man and woman in the street. I have to emphasize it here because some scientists and philosophers, in essence, deny it. I emphasize this feature because it lies outside what materialist reductionists include in their causal schemes. But as soon as I say it, it is obviously true. It is crucial to a religious view of life, and an extraordinary thought is that *ethics can be causally effective only because of the detailed nature of physics*, because physics is controlling the way that electrons and molecules flow in our neurons and enable our thoughts. So one of the really interesting questions is, Which aspect of physics allows this to happen? And how different could physics be and still allow this? This study leads to the anthropic conundrum that I have already mentioned.

Physics and Purpose

A further important point about physics in relation to the science and religion debate is that, despite what any physicist may explicitly tell you or implicitly imply, physics as it currently stands is causally incomplete. It is not able to describe all the forces in action shaping what happens in the world around us. I would like to illustrate this with a pair of spectacles.

Physics cannot explain the curve of the glass in the spectacles, because they have been shaped on purpose to fit my individual eyes. Now, the hierarchy of variables considered by physics contains quantities like momentum and energy, pressures and densities, and so on. But the vocabulary of physics has no variable corresponding to intention. As a result, physics cannot explain why these spectacles have their particular curvature. This is not a statement of vitalist belief. It is a simple statement of fact, which remains true irrespective of what your philosophy of mind may be. Physics today provides a causally incomplete theory of the world around us. It cannot describe all the causes acting to shape what happens in the real world.[22] For physics to be causally complete, at a minimum it would have to introduce some variables corresponding to intentions and rational plans. That would in turn involve introducing equations attempting to show how intentions form—in order to explain the curvature of the spectacles, the existence of motor cars, the structure of computers, and indeed the existence and nature of the building in which we are presently situated. None of these variables or equations exist in present-day physics, which therefore cannot comprehend the corresponding effects.

Furthermore, it can be argued that physics is simply causally incomplete; it cannot even in principle determine the outcomes of the actions of the human mind. To see the improbability of this claim, one can contemplate what is required from this viewpoint when placed in its proper cosmic context. The implication is that the particles that existed at the time of decoupling of the Cosmic Background Radiation in the early universe just happened to be placed so precisely as to make it inevitable that, fourteen billion years later, human beings would exist and Crick and Watson would discover DNA, Townes would conceive of the laser, and Witten would develop M-theory. In my view, this is absurd. It is inconceivable that truly random quantum fluctuations in the inflationary era—the supposed source of later emergent structure—can have had implicitly coded in them the future inevitability of the *Mona Lisa*, Nelson's victory at Trafalgar, and Einstein's 1905 theory of relativity. Such later creations of the mind are clearly not random; on the contrary, they exhibit high levels of order embodying sophisticated understandings of painting, military tactics, and physics, respectively, which cannot possibly have directly arisen from random initial data. This proposal simply does not account for the origin of such higher-level order.

It is far more likely that the later higher-level outcomes were not the consequences of specific aspects of the initial data, even though they arose out of them. Conditions at the time of decoupling of the Cosmic Background Radiation in the early universe fourteen billion years ago were such as to lead to life and, ultimately, minds that are autonomously effective, able to create higher-level order without any fine dependence on initial data. The higher-level understandings in the mind were not specifically implied by the initial data in the early universe, neither were their physical outcomes, such as television sets and cell phones. This development of such mental abilities is possible if there is a large-scale context that is causally channeling the development of fluctuations "in the right direction" for them to eventually contribute to the existence of minds creating such things as the *Mona Lisa*. This channeling is provided by the combination of the nature of the underlying possibility landscape and the developing order accumulating through Darwinian evolutionary processes, selecting between variations provided by chance effects on the large scale and quantum uncertainty on the small scale. Random variation followed by selection is a powerful mechanism that can accumulate biological order and information related to specific purposes. A key feature here is that while this process of variation and selection proceeds in a physical way, it also involves abstract patterns that are not physical phenomena; selection processes operating in biological systems develop in such a way as to recognize abstract patterns, which then become part of the causal processes in operation.[23] Overall, this mechanism is the way top-down action shapes the lower-level components to fulfill their higher-level roles. The selection process utilizes higher-level information about the environment—which may or may not correspond to coarse-grained variables—to shape the micro-level outcomes.

Limits of Science

There are many areas of concern for humans, of which only a subset are within the ambit of science. Outside of this ambit are crucially important areas—in particular, ethics, aesthetics, metaphysics, and meaning. They are outside the competence of science because no scientific experiment can determine any of them. Science can help illuminate some of their aspects, but is fundamentally unable to touch their core. Because of the very nature of science, there are absolute boundaries to what science can ever do.

Science and Ethics

A great deal of confusion surrounds this area, particularly in the case of ethics, which is outside the competence of science because no experiment can say that an act is good or bad. There are no units of good and bad, no measurements of so many "milli-Hitlers." Ethics is simply an area that science cannot handle.[24] Science depends on and supports some basic virtues, such as respecting the data, telling the truth, and so on, but this does not begin to touch real ethical issues dealing with the relative importance of ends and means, how to deal with conflicting interests, how to balance outcomes against principles, and so on. They simply do not help as regards real-world ethical dilemmas.

However, sociobiology and evolutionary psychology produce arguments that claim to give complete explanations as to the origin of our ethical views. There are many problems with those attempts, the first being that they do not explain ethics, they explain it away. If the true origin of our ethical beliefs lay in evolutionary biology, ethics would be completely undermined, because once you understood this you would no longer necessarily believe that you had to follow its precepts. You could choose to buck the evolutionary imperative. The second problem is that this is a typical fundamentalist argument that looks at some of the causes in operation and ignores others; it simply leaves out of consideration two other important parts of the equation, namely, social effects embodied in culture (which some sociologists and anthropologists with equal fundamentalist vehemence claim are all that matter) and personal choice.

The third problem is that if you did follow those precepts, you would rapidly end up in very dangerous territory, namely, the domain of social Darwinism. That has been one of the most evil movements in the history of humanity, causing far more deaths than any other ideology.[25] The fact that I am able to say it is evil shows that standards of ethics exist outside of those provided by evolutionary biology. A substantial literature has emerged on the evolutionary rise of altruism, which one might claim offers the hope of providing a basis for a positive ethic from a scientific basis. But first, the mere fact that such behavior occurs does not show it is *right*; so that fact does not provide a basis for ethics (all sorts of other behavior occurs too: one needs a criterion from outside of science to decide which is right and which wrong). Second, as a historical fact the influence of evolutionary theory on ethics has, in practice, been to provide theoretical support for eugenics and social Darwinism, not for any movement of caring for others. The historical record is quite clear.

Challenging evolutionary biologists who still maintain that their science can provide a basis for ethics, despite these arguments, is very simple. If a scientist says, "Look, science can handle ethics," say to them, "Tell me, what does science say should be done about Iraq today? And tell me what science says ethically about Israel and Palestine?" You will get a deafening silence, because the simple fact is that science cannot handle ethical questions. Ethical values, crucial for our individual and social lives, have to come from a value-based philosophical stance or a meaning-providing religious position. They cannot be justified by rationality alone, much less by science.

Aesthetics, Metaphysics, and Meaning

Similarly, aesthetic—the criteria of beauty—is also outside the boundaries of science. No scientific experiment can determine that something is beautiful or ugly, for these concepts are not scientific. The same is true for metaphysics and meaning. Thus, there are major areas of life, incredibly important to humanity, that cannot be encompassed in science. They are the proper domain of philosophy, of religion, of art, and so on, but not of science.

Why are there these boundaries? Because experimental science deals with the generic, the universal, in very restricted circumstances. It works in circumstances so tightly prescribed that effects are repeatable. Most things that are of real value in human life are not repeatable. They are individual events that may have crucial meaning for individuals and for humanity in the course of history, but each occurs only once. So repeatable science does not encompass either all that is important or all that can reasonably be called "knowledge."

Emotions and Values, Faith and Hope

Furthermore, we have the tension among rationality, emotion, faith, and hope. Some science-based worldviews claim, in essence, that reason is all that is needed for life, while emotion, faith, and hope simply get in the way of rationally desirable decisions; this is a false view. Reasoning things out and making decisions purely on a rational basis is not possible. First, we need values to guide our rational decisions, but these cannot be arrived at scientifically or rationally. Second, in order to live our lives we need faith and hope, because we always have inadequate information. It is a part of daily life that when we make important decisions like whom to marry, whether to take a new job, or whether to move to a new city, they are always to a considerable degree guided by emotion, and in the end have to be concluded on the basis of partial information.

A lot of choices are thus based on faith and hope, faith about how things will be, hope that it will work out all right. This is true even in science. Scientists set up research groups to look at string theory, particle physics, and so on in the belief that they will be able to obtain useful advances when their grant applications have been funded. They do not *know* that they will make those steps forward. It is a belief; it is a hope. Embedded thus in the very foundations even of science is a human structure of faith and hope.[26] Furthermore, scientists actually carry out these enterprises because of the associated emotions and values that guide their actions. For example, the desire to understand is an emotion that underlies much of science; similarly, setting up a scientific project is an exercise in hope.

Faith, of course, extends to the religious sphere. The science and religion dialogue can provide a basis for faith that is compatible with religious belief.[27] These discussions contradict various writings that claim science is in conflict with religion, writings that are philosophically ill-informed.

Balancing Reason, Emotion, and Ethics

It is crucial to understand that our minds act, as it were, as an arbiter among three tendencies guiding our actions: first, what rationality suggests is the best course of action, the cold calculus of more and less, the economically most beneficial choice; second, what emotion sways us to do, the way that feels best, what we would like to do; and third, what our values tell us we ought to do, the ethically best option, the right thing to do. These tendencies are each distinct from each other, and in competition to gain the upper hand. Sometimes they may agree as to the best course of action, but often they will not. Our personal responsibility is to choose between them, making the best choice we can between these conflicting calls, with our best wisdom and integrity, and on the basis of the limited data available.

This shows where value choices come in and help guide our actions. Rationality can help decide which course of action will be most likely to promote specific ethical goals when we have made these value choices, but the choices themselves, the ethical system, must come from outside the pure rationality of rigorous proof, and certainly from outside science. As emphasized before, science cannot provide the basis of ethics. A deep religious worldview is crucial here and is essential to our well-being and proper fulfillment, because ethics and meaning are deeply intertwined. Humans have a great yearning for meaning, and ethics embodies those meanings and guides our actions in accordance with them.

Moral Realism and the Nature of Ethics

I take the position of moral realism, which argues that we do not invent ethics, but discover it. A whole sociological school suggests that we invent ethics; it is created by society. That route ends up in total relativism, where it is impossible to say that any act is evil, for it is a simple fact that different social groups have different ethical beliefs. All you can say from this standpoint is that some people have different socially determined values than others; nothing can be labeled as bad or evil. It is simply that Hitler and Churchill were told different things by their mothers. Neither man did anything wrong, for "wrong" has no universal meaning. If, however, you believe truly that some acts are good and some are bad, you have to recognize the ability to distinguish good and bad, and that is a statement of ethical realism. We don't invent ethics, rather we discover it, in much the same way as we discover mathematics, which has a universal character that is the same everywhere in the universe, invariant across time and space.[28]

Kenosis

I am talking here about deep ethics, which is different from the shallow ethics on which everybody agrees and that sociobiology can explain. What is deep ethics? It is *kenosis*: self-emptying, or giving up, or self-sacrifice, which is deeply embedded in all the religious traditions of the world. It is the core of Christianity; the suffering on the cross is a kenotic, self-sacrificial giving up on behalf of humanity.[29] I believe that each of the major world religions has a spiritual tradition that believes seriously and deeply in a kenotic ethics. The real division is not in this ethical sphere. The division lies between the fundamentalists and the nonfundamentalists, irrespective of whether they are within the same religion/faith group or not. The nonfundamentalists can get on with each other irrespective of their faith positions, and, I suggest, agree on the deep nature of ethics, whichever faith they come from.

Existence and Evidence

One of the most common errors in discussing science and philosophy is mixing up existence with knowledge of existence, ontology with epistemology. Things can exist though we cannot conclusively demonstrate that they exist. There is a very simple example of this from cosmology. Since the universe is fourteen billion years old, the furthest that we can see in crude terms is fourteen billion light years. On most models of the universe, there is material beyond that distance that we cannot see now and indeed that humans never will be able to see. That does not mean these stars and galaxies do not exist; they are simply beyond where we can interact with them, so we cannot conclusively demonstrate their existence by any kind of observation. But there is a very old human tendency, embodied in theories ranging from logical positivism to extreme relativism, to think that things don't exist if we can't *prove* they exist. Not so. This is simply another form of human hubris.

At a deeper level, our inability to scientifically prove the existence of morality or meaning does not prove they are meaningless concepts. The nature of existence goes way beyond the material world. Hints of other levels of existence are there in the existence of physical laws and the discovery of mathematical reality, as well as in the multiple natures of consciousness and the experience of moral dilemmas. But to recognize these aspects and see their implications, you have to be open to the possible existence of deeper layers of reality, to be sensitive to hints of transcendence embedded in everyday physical existence.[30]

Discernment

This sensitivity leads to the question of discernment. The problem is that throughout history many people have felt strongly that they were being led by God, but you can tell by their actions that in some cases they were being led not by the God of Jesus, but rather by some other God or by their own self-centeredness. Many evils have resulted; inter alia, the Crusades and the Inquisition were carried out in the name of God, and the policy of apartheid was supported by a group of churches. The crucial issue is discernment, the testing of such urgings to see if they are really the true voice. A clear link with science is present here, because the strength of science comes through its process of testing to see if its conclusions are true. The real challenge for us is to test our spiritual leadings for their veracity, and to relate this to the transcendent.[31]

The Whole Picture

Conflict between science and religion comes when people see things in a partial way, thinking that part of the picture is the whole picture. We need to listen to what both science and religion can tell us in order to understand the whole. Science can help us understand many aspects of reality and, in particular, see the fine-tuning in physics that allows our existence. That understanding can be very precise, and it can make a huge impression. Our broader experience can give us a relation to spiritual issues with many dimensions. In terms of the beauty of things, I get that by walking in the mountains every Saturday and looking at birds, trees, waterfalls, flowers, clouds, the sea, and all the rest of it. In terms of religious experience, it can be found in the gathered Quaker Meeting for worship. All these aspects of experience, as well as scientific understandings, need to be taken seriously.

True Consilience

A broadly based science and religion dialogue has the potential to provide a deeper and more profound consilience than is possible any other way, because it can probe root causes and meaning in a way that science by itself cannot do. It can link science to ethics and meaning (telos) and even to aesthetics. In doing so, it can keep alive the awareness of the spiritual dimension of life in the face of scientific certainties—from the viewpoint of faith, deepening our wonder and awe as we appreciate the mechanisms by which our life has been created and supported.[32] This awareness can be claimed to be the true nature of spirituality: being profoundly aware of all these dimensions of existence, appreciating them all and their interconnections, replacing the "nothing but" of reductionism by wonder, reverence, and awe.

Embracing the Whole

In many areas we do not have any answers. We always need to remember that what we can know about both science and religion is limited, but both science and religion are important to being a fully rounded human being. We need to incorporate both of them. Even if you are not a scientist, it is worth trying to find out about science because it tells us so much. But this does not mean having to deny religion or, indeed, humanity. The religious life adds an enormously important dimension to humanity, individually and collectively, when approached in a nonfundamentalist way.

Multiple Views

One of the significant issues, of course, is the multiple views of the nature of ultimate reality offered by religion. Does this discord of views show there is no such thing? In my view, no; there are bound to be multiple understandings of the transcendent, depending on our own life experience and expertise.[33] Indeed, this kind of multiple viewpoint already occurs in science: Penrose, for example, shows very clearly how they occur in the physical sciences and in mathematics.[34] Many different representations of the same object are possible. The dualities of quantum theory also illustrate this issue; the same physical object can have quite different effects and manifestations.

Applied Values

Also at issue is how applied science impacts lives—for example, in terms of biotechnology issues such as cloning, values in environmental decisions, production of weapons, and so on. What is the nature of the values that guide our decisions? There is a need for ethical values, which science cannot provide; it can only come from religious and philosophical positions, and can fruitfully be explored by the science and religion dialogue. Consider the possibility, perhaps, of a panel of religious representatives—experts, maybe, in the field of science and religion and reflective of the various faith traditions, who might provide ethical guidance on crucial issues that a panel of scientists cannot. Such a panel, for example, could be attached to the United Nations.

Underlying this proposal is a core belief that the spiritual wings of the great world religions have a common core of ethical values that can be used to provide guidance in practical situations, that, as indicated above, they all agree on kenosis as an underlying basis for deep ethics. In my view, ample evidence exists that this agreement is indeed the case.

Integrative Viewpoints

Through all these discussions, the science and religion debate can be a good force in the development of truly multidisciplinary studies: in the sciences themselves and also integrating them into a cohesive viewpoint compatible with the humanities, arts, and well-considered philosophy. This debate not only can help develop worldviews that can accommodate the pragmatic nature of science but also identify the kinds of deeper issues regarding existence and meaning that can be encountered in spiritual and religious worldviews. Thus it can explore the deep nature of reality in a way that helps deepen the understanding of the religious and spiritual nature of existence, also taking physical reality and science into account. This approach is important in its own right; it is what helps create deeper meaning in our lives. Additionally, as indicated above, this debate is important in terms of its outcomes. Dehumanizing views of our nature lead, inevitably, to the dehumanizing treatment of people. This issue alone makes the science and religion dialogue an important contribution to life today.

Notes

1. J. Haught, *Science and Religion: From Conflict to Conversation* (Mahwah, N.J.: Paulist Press, 1995); I. Barbour, *Religion and Science: Historical and Contemporary Issues* (San Francisco: Harper, 1997).
2. N. Murphy, *Theology in an Age of Scientific Reasoning* (Ithaca: Cornell University Press, 1990).
3. W. Paden, *Interpreting the Sacred* (Boston: Beacon Press, 1992).
4. K. Ward, *Defending the Soul* (Oxford: One World, 1992); J. Bowker, *Is God a Virus?* (London: SPCK, 1995).
5. G. F. R. Ellis, "The Thinking Underlying the New 'Scientific' Worldviews," in *Evolutionary and Molecular Biology*, ed. R. Russell, W. Stoeger, and F. Ayala, 251–80 (Castel Gandolfo: Vatican Observatory/Berkeley: The Centre for Theology and the Natural Sciences, 1998).
6. J. D. Barrow and F. J. Tipler, *The Anthropic Cosmological Principle* (Oxford: Clarendon Press, 1986).
7. M. Rees, *Our Cosmic Habitat* (New York: Basic Books, 2001); M. Rees, *Just Six Numbers: The Deep Forces that Shape the Universe* (Princeton: Princeton University Press, 2003); L. Susskind, *The Cosmic Landscape: String Theory and the Illusion of Intelligent Design* (New York: Little Brown, 2005).
8. Susskind, *The Cosmic Landscape.*
9. G. F. R. Ellis, "The Theology of the Anthropic Principle," in *Quantum Cosmology and the Laws of Nature*, ed. R. J. Russell, N. Murphy and C. J. Isham, 367–406 (Castel Gandolfo: Vatican Observatory/Berkeley: The Centre for Theology and the Natural Sciences, 1993); N. Murphy and G. Ellis, *On the Moral Nature of the Universe* (Minneapolis: Fortress Press, 1995).

10. Rees, *Our Cosmic Habitat*; Rees, *Just Six Numbers.*
11. Susskind, *Cosmic Landscape.*
12. G. F. R. Ellis, U. Kirchner and W. Stoeger, "Multiverses and Physical Cosmology," *Monthly Notices Royal Astronomical Society* 347: 921-36
13. M. Gardner, *Are Universes Thicker Than Blackberries?* (New York: W. W. Norton, 2004).
14. S. Pinker, *The Blank Slate* (London: Penguin, 2003).
15. P. Berger, *A Rumor of Angels: Modern Society and the Rediscovery of the Supernatural* (New York: Doubleday, 1990).
16. M. Donald, *A Mind So Rare: The Evolution of Human Consciousness* (New York: W. W. Norton, 2001), 29, 36.
17. Author inter alia of *Elbow Room: The Varieties of Free Will Worth Wanting* (Cambridge, Mass: MIT Press, 1984) and *Freedom Evolves* (New York: Penguin Books, 2004).
18. Donald, *A Mind So Rare,* 31, 45.
19. G. F. R. Ellis and J. A. Toronchuk, "Neural Development: Affective and Immune System Influences," in *Consciousness and Emotion: Agency, Conscious Choice, and Selective Perception*, ed. R. D. Ellis and N. Newton, 81–119 (Amsterdam: John Benjamins, 2005).
20. G. F. R. Ellis, "On the Nature of Emergent Reality," in *The Re-emergence of Emergence*, ed. P. Clayton and P. C. W. Davies (Oxford: Oxford University Press, 2004); G. F. R. Ellis, "Physics and the Real World," *Foundations of Physics* 36, no. 2 (2006)
21. Ellis, "Physics and the Real World"; J. Roederer, *Information and Its Role in Nature* (Berlin: Springer, 2005).
22. Ellis, "Physics and the Real World."
23. Roederer, *Information and Its Role in Nature.*
24. Murphy and Ellis, *On the Moral Nature of the Universe.*
25. R. Weikart, *From Darwin to Hitler: Evolutionary Ethics, Eugenics, and Racism in Germany* (New York: Palgrave Macmillan, 2004).
26. R. P. Crease, "The Paradox of Trust in Science," *Physics World* 17 (March 2004): 18.
27. A. Peacocke, T*heology for a Scientific Age: Being and Becoming—Natural, Human, and Divine* (Minneapolis: Fortress Press, 1993); K. Ferguson, *The Fire in the Equations: Science, Religion, and the Search for God* (Minneapolis: Fortress Press, 1994); Murphy and Ellis, *On the Moral Nature of the Universe*; J. Polkinghorne, *Belief in God in an Age of Science* (New Haven, CT: Yale University Press, 1998).
28. Murphy and Ellis, *On the Moral Nature of the Universe.*
29. Ellis, "The Theology of the Anthropic Principle."
30. Nhat Hanh, Thich, *The Miracle of Mindfulness* (London: Rider, 1987).
31. J. Hick, *An Interpretation of Religion: Human Responses to the Transcendent* (New Haven: Yale University Press, 1992).
32. Nhat Hanh, *Miracle of Mindfulness.*
33. Paden, *Interpreting the Sacred.*
34. R. Penrose, *The Road to Reality: A Complete Guide to the Laws of the Universe* (London: Jonathan Cape, 2003).

2

Does "Science and Religion" Matter?

JOHN POLKINGHORNE

LET ME BEGIN by asking a related question: "Does science matter?" You might be tempted to answer, "Of course it does, because of all the things that it gives us. Without science there would be no television, no Internet, not even a refrigerator." But that would be to confuse science with its lusty offspring, technology. The latter takes the discoveries of science and uses them to produce inventions. Technology is about getting things done, but science itself is concerned with something different. Its goal is not power, but understanding. Doing scientific research is hard work. There is much wearisome routine, as there is in any worthwhile activity, and moments of frustration and disappointment occur as well as moments of insight. The reason scientists stick at it is that they want to understand the world.

And science has been wonderfully successful in that task. Not only can we make sense of many of the processes that affect our everyday lives but we can understand strange and counterintuitive regimes whose nature is very different from that of everyday experience and that have no direct impact upon it. We have successfully explored the strange and elusive subatomic world of quantum theory and the vast domain of cosmic curved spacetime. Not only can we understand what is going on at the present time but we can also comprehend what was happening in the remote past, when things were very different, so that we can trace the history of life on Earth over three to four billion years, and understand the fourteen-billion-year history of the universe itself.

These achievements are very impressive, and they are to be taken with the utmost seriousness. Yet science has purchased this great success by the modesty of its ambition. It operates in a self-limited domain. Science does not ask and answer every question we might have about the human encounter with reality. Essentially it restricts itself to dealing with the question of how things happen. The center of its concern is the natural processes of the world. In answering its chosen question, science treats reality as an "it," an object that can be manipulated and put to the experimental test, kicked around to see how it responds, and torn apart to find out what it is made of. Science deals with the generality of things, concentrating mostly on phenomena that are repeatable, and avoiding—as much as possible—thinking about one-time events. These characteristics have furnished science with its great secret weapon, experiment—the technique of testing that has enabled it to make such great progress in its chosen area of inquiry.

Yet we all know that there are other great swaths of human encounters, with reality that fall outside these limits. There is the realm of the personal, where our meeting is with a "Thou" rather than an "it." In this sphere of experience, testing has to give way to trusting. If I am always setting little traps to see if you are my friend, I shall soon destroy the possibility of friendship between us. In this realm of the personal, all moments of experience are unique, for their quality is unrepeatable. We never hear a Beethoven quartet the same way twice, even if we replay the same disc. Exciting and illuminating as the discoveries of science undoubtedly are, in this transscientific personal realm most of the deepest satisfactions of human life are to be found. And many, including the present speaker, wish to testify to a yet more profound realm of human experience in which we encounter the transpersonal reality of God. Here, attaining knowledge demands attitudes of awe, reverence, and obedience, for it is just a fact of the spiritual life that "You shall not put the Lord your God to the test."

"How" is not the only question to ask of reality. There is the complementary question "why." Is there something going on in what is happening? Do meaning and purpose lie behind what is occurring? Science has bracketed out questions of this kind, but human beings should not be beguiled into believing that this implies that in some curious way these questions are meaningless or irrelevant. In fact, we know quite the contrary, for they raise issues that are vital for an adequate quest for truth.

Those who are imbued with a thirst for understanding through and through—a desire that is extremely natural to the scientist—will find that this thirst will not be quenched by self-limited science alone. Religious insight offers us the prospect of finding a deeper level of understanding than that which we can get from scientific explanation on its own. That is why "science and religion" matters. Combining these two great human encounters with reality offers the prospect of a more profound understanding than either could offer by itself. This synthesis is perfectly natural, since science and religion in their intrinsic relationship are friends and not foes. This is because they share a cousinly connection in the common search for truth attainable through motivated belief. People sometimes fail to see this in the case of religion, because they have an erroneous picture that faith is a matter of believing impossible things simply on the basis of being told to do so by some unquestionable authority. If that were the case I could not be a man of faith, for I do not believe that God calls us to commit intellectual suicide. We are to make full use of the divine gift of reason. I frequently try to help my unbelieving but inquiring friends to see that I have *motivations* for my religious beliefs, just as I have motivations for my scientific beliefs. Of course, the character of these motivations differs in the two cases, just as the subject matter of the beliefs differs in the way that we have just discussed. But science and religion matter and interact with each other precisely because they are both concerned with the human quest for truthful knowledge of reality.

"How" and "why" are two different questions, but the manner in which we answer them has to fit together in some consonant fashion. If I said that my purpose was to make a cup of tea and the way in which I was going to do so was by putting the kettle in the refrigerator, you would rightly doubt the sincerity of my remarks. Science cannot answer religion's questions, and religion cannot answer science's questions, but the two sets of answers have to fit together in some consonant way. That is one reason that a continuing and fruitful dialogue is taking place between the two, a conversation that I believe to be in a particularly lively and helpful state today. Some questions also arise from experience relating to one form of insightful inquiry, but whose answering carries us into the domain of the other. One may call these "metaquestions," questions that take us beyond our starting point. I want to end this brief chapter by looking at two such metaquestions.

The first is so simple a question that we seldom stop to ask it. Nevertheless, I believe that it is significant and one that we should take very seriously. It is simply this: "Why is science possible at all? Why can we understand the physical world so deeply?" It is scarcely surprising that we can understand the world in the everyday kind of way that is obviously necessary for our survival within it. Yet the development of modern science has shown that our human ability far exceeds anything that could reasonably be considered as simply an evolutionary necessity, or a happy spin-off from that necessity. We can penetrate the secrets of the subatomic realm of quantum theory and make maps of the vast structure of the universe, both regimes of no direct practical impact upon us, and both exhibiting properties that seem very strange in relation to our ordinary ways of thinking.

In fact, the matter is yet more curious, for it also turns out that mathematics is the key to unlocking these scientific secrets. In fundamental physics it is an actual technique of discovery to look for equations that have about them the unmistakable character of mathematical beauty, for time and again we find that it is only equations of this kind that will prove to be the basis for theories whose long-term fruitfulness convinces us that they are indeed descriptions of physical reality. A very great physicist, Paul Dirac, once said that the quest for mathematical beauty was "a very profitable religion" to hold.[1] Dirac made his many great discoveries by a lifelong and highly successful search of just this kind.

When we use abstract mathematics in this way, as a guide to physical discovery, something very odd is happening. After all, mathematics is pure thought, and what could it be that links that thought to the structure of the physical world around us? From the point of view of science, the rational transparency and rational beauty of the universe are simply astonishing pieces of luck, enabling the successes of fundamental physics and affording researchers the reward of a deep sense of wonder at the marvelous patterns revealed to their inquiries. Religious belief in the universe as a creation, and of human beings as persons made in the image of the Creator, offers a profound understanding of the origin of these scientific experiences. The reason of our minds (mathematics) and the rational order of the world (the beautiful equations of physics) relate to each other because they have a common origin in the reason of the Creator. The universe, in its deep order, appears to us as a world shot through with signs of mind precisely because the Mind of God is indeed the source of its rational beauty. This combination of the insights of science and religion makes intelligible a remarkable human capacity that otherwise might have seemed merely fortuitous.

A second kind of metaquestion takes us in the direction of ethics: what is the right use of the capacities that science places at our disposal? Science itself gives us knowledge, and that is surely always a welcome gift, since knowledge is a better basis for decision than ignorance. Technology takes that knowledge and turns it into the power to get things done. That is a more ambiguous gift, since not everything that can be done should be done. We stand, therefore, in need of a third gift, which is wisdom, the power to choose the good and refuse the bad, and to know which is which. Religion does not have a monopoly on wisdom, but the faith traditions are reservoirs of much experience of reaching ethical decisions, accumulated over many centuries. Attention to ethical questions is an important component in the dialogue between science and religion.

Deep issues can be involved in moral argument. Take the currently contentious case of research using embryonic stem cells. Virtually everyone agrees that human persons are not to be used instrumentally. In Kant's famous formulation, they are always ends and never means. If a very early embryo is already a full human person, with all the moral status that implies, it would be as unthinkable to destroy it in order to extract its stem cells as it would be to remove the heart from a living person in order to implant into another. But before fourteen days, the embryo has no intrinsic structure beyond the DNA in each of its undifferentiated cells. Is it really already a person, or is that status something that it will grow into in the course of its development? If the latter is the case, its instrumental use for very serious purposes, unlikely to be attainable by a nonembryonic route, becomes an ethically conceivable possibility. Different theological traditions answer this question in different ways, and my purpose is not on this occasion to attempt to adjudicate the matter. I simply want to emphasize that the human quest for right ethical decisions has a complexity that demands the cooperative sharing of insights between science and religion.

Does "science and religion" matter? Of course it does, because it is an indispensable element in the great human quest for truth. I am both a physicist and a priest, and I am grateful for the way in which my experiences in science and religion give me a kind of two-eyed perspective onto reality. With this binocular vision I believe that I can see more than I could with either eye on its own.

Note

1. Quoted in M. Longair, *Theoretical Concepts in Physics* (Cambridge: Cambridge University Press, 1984), 7.

3

The Science and Religion Dialogue

WHY IT MATTERS

HOLMES ROLSTON III

I ONCE STARTED a science and religion class with the claim that these are the two most important things in the world. A student promptly objected: "No, Professor, you are wrong: that's sex and money." I convinced him otherwise by the time the semester was over. But I am still trying to convince most of the world. Science is the first fact of modern life, and religion is the perennial carrier of meaning. Seen in depth and in terms of their long-range personal and cultural impacts, science and religion are the two most important forces in today's world.

Here are six reasons why the dialogue is vital:

1. *Science cannot teach us what we need most to know about nature—that is, how to value it.* That claim might seem too bold, but I do make it in a box essay, "What Is Our Duty to Nature?," that I was invited to write by concerned biologists, authors of a widely used general biology textbook. So the claim is now confronting tens of thousands of biology students across the nation.[1] Science does teach us natural history. Science gives us great powers for the improvement of human life through technology. But science limps when it comes to values. What to make of nature, looking to the evolutionary past? What to make of nature, given our technological prowess? Whether we wish a managed nature, and who will be the managers and how they ought to manage—none of these are questions answered by science.

2. *Science cannot teach us what we most need to know about culture—that is, how to value it.* That is the other side of the question we were just addressing. Science has a hard back but a soft underbelly. We modern humans, increasingly competent about making our way through the natural world, have been decreasingly confident about its values, its meanings.

The correlation is not accidental. One of the proverbs of my country rearing was, "The faster a blind horse runs, the sooner it will perish." It is hard to discover meaning in a world where value appears only at the human touch, hard to locate meaning when engulfed with sheer instrumentality, whether of artifacts or natural resources.

The doctrine of original sin is said to be the only empirically verifiable teaching in my Presbyterian heritage. Since 9/11 and Enron, we hardly need convinced that, globally and domestically, we confront value questions as sharp and as painful as ever. Consummate capitalism, though it may raise the living standards of many, seems also to make the rich richer and the poor poorer. One of our national goals seems to be ever-escalating consumption, funded by ever-smarter science. But my Shenandoah Valley ancestors thought of consumption as a disease. Power corrupts, and absolute power corrupts absolutely. Lord Acton was absolutely right.

3. *Science increasingly opens up religious questions.* This is quite contrary to the more frequent claim that science eliminates religion. If one looks closely, there are religious dimensions in the thought of otherwise secular thinkers. I have time only for two; I could cite twenty. I will use two well-placed Boston scientists.

Stephen Jay Gould finds Earth the scene of "wonderful life," even if this is just "chance riches."[2] Indeed, in the last words he wrote, he was moved to use the word "holy": "Something almost unspeakably holy—I don't know how else to say this—underlies our discovery and confirmation of the actual details that made our world and also, in realms of contingency, assured the minutiae of its construction in the manner we know, and not in any one of a trillion other ways, nearly all of which would not have included the evolution of a scribe to record the beauty, the fascination, and the mystery."[3] E. O. Wilson, a secular humanist, ever insistent that he can find no divinity in, with, or under nature, still exclaims, with emphasis: "The flower in the crannied wall—it *is* a miracle."[4] "The biospheric membrane that covers Earth, and you and me, . . . is the miracle we have been given."[5] Maybe these code words "miracle," "sacred," and "holy" are just rhetoric; maybe they are provocative. But I suspect even these secularists are tugged by a deeper undertow than they realize in their encounters with the archaic orders.

The secular—this present empirical epoch, this phenomenal world, studied by science—does not eliminate the sacred after all; to the contrary, the secular evolves into the sacred.

4. *The future of religion depends on the dialogue.* Many of my professors taught me that science and religion were independent areas of life, rather like law and poetry, each with their own integrity, but that to relate the two was to try to integrate incommensurables. They were half right, but that half-truth taken for the whole is quite wrong. The religion that is married to science today will be a widow tomorrow, so they said. The sciences in their multiple theories and forms come and go. Physics today is very different from the physics I was taught half a century ago. Biology in the year 2050 may be as different from the biology of today as the religion of today is from the religion of 1850.

But the religion that is divorced from science today will leave no offspring tomorrow. From here onward, no religion can reproduce itself in succeeding generations unless it has faced the operations of nature and the claims about human nature with which science confronts us.

The problem is somewhat like the one that confronts a living biological species fitting itself into its niche in the changing environment. There must be a good fit for survival, and yet overspecialization is an almost certain route to extinction. Religion that has too thoroughly accommodated to any science will soon be obsolete. It needs to keep its autonomous integrity and resilience. Yet religion cannot live without fitting into the intellectual world that is its environment. Here, too, the fittest survive.

5. *Dialogue offers new opportunities for understanding and confronting suffering and evil.* Something stirs in the cold, mathematical beauty of physics, in the heated energies supplied by matter; there is life, and still later suffering subjects. Energy turns into pain. The capacity to suffer evolves as a complement to the capacity to survive. Across the whole of evolutionary history, renewed life comes by blasting the old. Environmental pressures shape life. Life is pressed by the storms, but it is pressed on by the storms, and environmental necessity is the mother of invention in life. Life is gathered up in the midst of its throes. Darwinians see this truth: there is a struggle for survival. But so far from making the world absurd, suffering is a key to the whole—not intrinsically, not as an end in itself, but as a transformative principle, transvalued into its opposite. Darwinians see dark clouds; Christians see the silver lining.

We begin to see the sacred character of life in its struggling beauty. Experiences of the power of survival, of new life rising out of the old, of the transformative character of suffering, of good resurrected out of evil, are quite forcefully those for which the theory of God has come to provide the most plausible hypothesis. I call this "cruciform creation." The perennial regeneration of life in the biological sciences is a precursor of the redemption of life offered in the religions. In both nature and culture there is something divine about the power to suffer through to something higher.

Earth is a kind of providing ground, where the life epic is lived on in the midst of its perpetual perishing. Life persists because it is provided for in the evolutionary and ecological Earth systems. Life is lived in grace through the besetting storm, green pastures, and the valley of the shadow of death. Today we say, life is generated "at the edge of chaos." Yesterday, John said, "The light shines in the darkness, and the darkness has not overcome it" (John 1:5).

6. *The dialogue between science and religion matters because the future of Earth depends on it.* I've been lucky that my own personal agenda, figuring nature out, has during my lifetime turned out to be the world agenda, figuring out the human place on the planet. Living locally led me to think globally. In that sense my autobiography has been writ large in the Earth agenda. I did not want to live a denatured life; it turns out that humans neither can nor ought to denature their planet. But my sense of wonder turned to horror when I encountered the oncoming environmental crisis. No sooner did I discover that nature is grace than I found we were treating it disgracefully.

In the new millennium, the four principal, interrelated challenges are war and peace, population, development, and environment. Science alone cannot teach us what we most need to know about any of the four. Maybe religion does not have all the answers or even any easy answers, but it does offer a comprehensive worldview within which we might work out some answers. If anything at all on Earth is sacred, it must be this enthralling generativity that characterizes our home planet. If there is any holy ground, any land of promise, this promising Earth is it.

The biblical faith originated with a land ethic. Within the covenant, keeping the commandments, the Hebrew people entered a promised land. Justice is to run down like waters, and the land flows with milk and honey.

That blessing can be received only if the land is inhabited justly and charitably. No people can live in harmony with their landscape, in a sustainable relationship with their natural resources, unless there is social justice. The Land of Promise is now the Planet of Promise.

Our planetary crisis is one of spiritual information: not so much how to sustain development, much less how to escalate consumption, but to use the Earth with justice and charity. Science cannot take us there; religion perhaps can. It is not simply what a society does to its slaves, women, blacks, minorities, handicapped, children, or future generations, but what it does to its fauna, flora, species, ecosystems, and landscapes that reveals the character of that society.

The astronaut Edgar Mitchell saw Earth from space as "a sparkling blue and white jewel . . . rising gradually like a small pearl in a thick sea of black mystery." Mitchell continued, "My view of our planet was a glimpse of divinity."[6] The secular autonomy that once seemed to banish any Presence turns out to veil a kind of haunting incompleteness. We need science talking to religion and religion talking to science to figure out who we are, where we are, and what we ought to do.

Notes

1. "What Is Our Duty to Nature?" in William K. Purves, David Sandava, Gordon H. Orians, and H. Craig Heller, *Life: The Science of Biology*, 7th ed. (Sunderland, Mass: Sinauer Associates, W. A. Freeman, 2004), 681.
2. Stephen Jay Gould, *Wonderful Life: The Burgess Shale and the Nature of History* (New York: Norton, 1989); Gould, "Chance Riches," *Natural History* 89, no. 11 (1980): 36–44.
3. Stephen Jay Gould, *The Structure of Evolutionary Theory* (Cambridge, Mass: Harvard University Press, 2002), 1342.
4. Edward O. Wilson, *The Diversity of Life* (Cambridge, Mass: Harvard University Press, 1992), 345.
5. Edward O. Wilson, *The Future of Life* (New York: Alfred A. Knopf, 2002), 21.
6. Edgar Mitchell, quoted in Kevin W. Kelley, ed., *The Home Planet* (Reading, Mass: Addison-Wesley, 1988), at photographs 42–45, 52.

Part 2
The International Context

4

Science and Religion

WHERE HAVE WE COME FROM AND WHERE ARE WE GOING?

JOHN POLKINGHORNE

THE CENTRAL THEME of this chapter is based on a talk that I gave at the inaugural meeting of the International Society for Science and Religion (ISSR) in Granada in 2002. Those involved in planning that meeting chose Granada for two important reasons. One was that southern Spain is close to the meeting point between two continents, Africa and Europe. The geographical location, therefore, symbolized the truly worldwide character that we believed would be so important and fruitful an aspect of the Society. The second reason was that, in the later Middle Ages, southern Spain was a place where adherents of three great religious traditions, Judaism, Christianity, and Islam, were able to intermingle and interact with each other. In fact, the later Middle Ages generally was in many ways a golden period for interfaith interaction. One has only to recite the names of Moses Maimonides, Thomas Aquinas, and Ibn Sina, and to recall all the fascinating threads that interconnect their thinking, to see that this was so. Sadly, this state of affairs did not last; it was brought to an end by political upheavals and expulsions and then the three Abrahamic faith traditions turned from each other and went their separate ways. The time has come to seek to reverse that process and to do so today in a fully worldwide way.

The talks at that first meeting were intended to view from a variety of perspectives future prospects for science and religion. It is famously difficult to define both subjects of this chapter, but let me first say something about how I understand the nature of science and the nature of religion. I see science as an activity of great value that has purchased its impressive success by the self-limited character of its ambition. It does not seek to consider all aspects of human encounter with the world, but it restricts itself to the realm of the impersonal, where reality is encountered as an "It," an object that can be manipulated and put to the empirical test—hence, the origin of science's great secret weapon, the experimental method. I am a theoretical physicist, but I gladly acknowledge the way in which my subject has developed through the empirically discerned nudge of nature. In that way, we have been led to ideas that would otherwise have been beyond our powers even to imagine; just think of the counterintuitive character of quantum theory. Much has been learned in this fashion, but we all know that there is another dimension to our encounter with the world, in which we meet reality personally—as a "Thou" and not as an "It"—and where true knowledge can be found only through trusting rather than through testing. Religion operates in this latter domain, and in particular in that transpersonal dimension, so differently described in detail by the different faith traditions but also clearly capable of being treated under the common rubric of a meeting with the reality of the Sacred.

The impersonal is the sphere of the repeatable, but the personal is the sphere of the unique. We never hear a piece of music exactly the same way twice, even if we replay the same disc. This unique significance of the unrepeatable is the reason that all the faith traditions have literature that acts normatively as scripture for that tradition; that is to say, as the record of those particular fundamental insights and experiences that are the basis of that tradition's understanding of the nature of the Sacred. Recognizing the indispensable role of the unique in religion, and of the foundational significance of scripture, also leads us to recognize another contrast between the practice of science and the continuing self-reflection of a religious community upon the character of its tradition.

Science is very much a matter of contemporary understanding. The cumulative character of the insights that it acquires in a well-winnowed field of investigation means that scientists can sit lightly to the discussions of the past. What was of value in those discussions will have been incorporated into the current account, and what did not prove to be of value will have been discarded on the way. What was worthwhile in the past is still accessible to us in the deposit of the present, so one does not need to look back to find it. The learned would describe this as being the synchronic character of scientific understanding. I am just an ordinary physicist, but I know much more about the universe than Isaac Newton ever did, great genius though he was. That is simply because I live three centuries later, and so I am heir to all the scientific discoveries that were made in those intervening years.

Things are different in religion. It is a diachronic subject, rather than a synchronic one. There is no presumptive superiority of the religious insights of the teachers of today over the insights of the sages of the past. The conversations of religion cannot simply be conducted in the present alone; they have to range over the centuries. In Christianity, my own faith tradition, the thought of figures such as Augustine and Aquinas and Luther and Calvin continues to engage the attention of twenty-first-century theologians. Of course, this does not mean that religion is simply in thrall to the past, caught in an antiquarian trap from which it cannot escape. New insights are certainly acquired, not least from interaction with new knowledge such as that which science has to offer.

I might by now have seemed to have indicated such a degree of difference between science and religion that one might wonder how mutual interaction might be possible at all. Therefore, let me emphasize in the strongest possible terms what I see as the fundamental common feature that they share together and which means not only that they can talk to each other, but that they *must* talk to each other. It is simply this: science and religion are both concerned with the search for truth. I realize, of course, that there are many today who would deny this claim, both in respect of science and in respect of religion. It is not possible for me in the course of this chapter to articulate an adequate reply to postmodern assertions of relativistic despair at our being able to gain any reliable knowledge of reality. Certainly, if such a response is to be made, whatever kind of realism it affirms will have to be qualified by the adjective "critical."

In science, the intertwining of theory and experiment, interpretation and experience, necessarily introduces a degree of circularity into the argument, but I believe that one can give reasons that this circularity is to be regarded as benign rather than as vicious. I am influenced here by Michael Polanyi, the only twentieth-century writer on these topics who was a distinguished scientist before he turned to philosophy. In his book *Personal Knowledge*, Polanyi tells us that he was writing to explain how he might commit himself to what he believed to be true, though he knew, in principle, that it might turn out to be false. I suppose a religious believer might say much the same, though, of course, realism in connection with religion's account of the veiled nature of the Sacred is as yet a more delicate and precarious matter. I believe that all of the world faith traditions, in their different ways, point to what in Christianity we call apophatic theology, the necessary acknowledgment of the limitation of any finite human mind in its ability to grasp the Infinite, to comprehend fully that ineffable mystery that lies at the heart of ultimate Reality. Yet I do not believe that any tradition finds itself simply driven to silence. There is a role for kataphatic utterance, the affirmation of those parts of truth that have been revealed to us. Subject to these provisos, we should recognize that truth is as important a matter for religion as it is for science. I also believe that both seek to attain their understanding of truth through the pursuit of motivated belief, though, as I have already indicated, the character of the motivations that are appropriate will be different in the two cases.

Yet there are also differences in the scope of the truth-seeking ambition to which science and religion respectively aspire. I have already said that I believe that science's success stems from the limited character of what it tries to achieve. Religion must strive for more. Since it is concerned with the Ground of all reality, it must seek to embrace all aspects of that reality. Religion, therefore, is seeking an overarching and comprehensive view. In that endeavor it must respect and take into account the insights of more specialized and limited inquiries, such as that of science. Here, then, is a primary reason for the necessity of interaction between science and religion.

Many of those who were engaged in this recent period of exchange between science and religion came from an intellectual background in physical science. Physicists, particularly those who work in the fundamental regimes of the very large and the very small, tend to be deeply impressed by the profound intelligibility and wonderful order of the universe. The world is rationally transparent to our inquiry, and rationally beautiful in its character, to a very remarkable degree. These facts give science both the possibility of its enterprise and the reward that accompanies its labors. Added to this is the property of the "unreasonable effectiveness of mathematics," which makes that abstract discipline the key with which to unlock the secrets of the physical universe.[1] It is a proven technique of discovery in fundamental physics to seek mathematically beautiful equations in the expectation, fulfilled time and again in our experience, that it is only equations with this character that will prove to have the long-term explanatory fruitfulness that persuades us of their verisimilitudinous nature. This is precisely how Einstein discovered general relativity and how Dirac discovered the relativistic equation of the electron. These properties of the deep intelligibility of the cosmos seem too striking to be treated as just happy accidents, requiring no further explanation. In consequence, many have suggested that they should be regarded as signs of the presence of a Divine Mind behind the order of the world. The claim made for this insight is that it is intellectually satisfying rather than logically coercive in its character. I, for one, certainly see the matter that way, as an illustration of how scientific experience and religious understanding can complement each other, without supposing that they entail each other.

Although life, as far as we know, only appeared in the universe when it was about ten billion years old, and self-conscious life after fourteen billion years, there is a real sense in which the cosmos was pregnant with the possibility of carbon-based life almost from the big bang onward. I am referring, of course, to the surprising collection of scientific insights into the fruitful particularity of our universe that are collected together under the rubric of the anthropic principle. It is not in the scope of this chapter to explicate the many considerations that indicate to us that this is so, nor to remind you of the many metascientific arguments that have raged about what significance might be attributed to it. At the very least, the belief that a divine Purpose lies behind the world provides an intellectually satisfying and economic explanation of why the universe has this "finely tuned" character embedded within its given physical fabric.

Of course, this inbuilt potentiality has been expressed and realized through the shuffling explorations of evolutionary process, both at the cosmic level and at the level of terrestrial biology. Although some biologists have been notably hostile to religion and have asserted that the role of contingency in evolution shows that the world is "meaningless" in its character, there have also been religiously minded biologists who have counterattacked with an alternative metascientific interpretation. The line they have taken can be traced back to the response to Darwin's ideas, expressed by some English clergymen very soon after the publication of *Origin of Species*. The key idea is to understand an evolutionary world as a creation allowed by its Creator *to make itself.* God neither produced a ready-made world nor imposed upon its history an eternally predetermined rigid form. Instead, the process of the universe is that of a continuously unfolding creativity, a kind of improvisation in which creatures participate together with their Creator. Such a world of freely developing fertility is a great good, but it has a necessary cost. The evolution of life has been driven by genetic mutation, but it is inevitable that the same processes that produce changes in germ cells leading to new forms of being will also, in somatic cells, produce changes leading to malignancy. The anguishing fact of the presence of cancer in creation is not due to the Creator's callousness or incompetence, but it is the necessary cost of a creation allowed to make itself. Here, I think, we see something of the potential power of the dialogue between science and religion, as the insight of the former assists the latter with one of its most perplexing problems: the presence of so much suffering in the world.

In my sector of the science and religion community, the topic that absorbed most of our attention in the last decade of the twentieth century was how we might properly think about divine providential action, considered in relation to what science has to say about the reliable process of the universe. It was widely recognized that contemporary science no longer gave a mechanical account of the clockwork world, in which all that happened was tame and predictable. On the contrary, the discoveries of quantum theory and chaos theory had revealed the presence of widespread intrinsic unpredictabilities present in physical process. Of course, questions of predictability are epistemological issues, while questions of causality are ontological issues. There is no logical entailment between epistemology and ontology, and what connection one chooses to make between them is a matter for philosophical argument and metaphysical decision. If you are a realist, as I am, you will suppose that the two are closely aligned, which can lead to a variety of possible conjectures about the open nature of the causal nexus of the world. It is not my present purpose to summarize that ten-year discussion, which was certainly fruitful but did not issue much in the way of generally agreed conclusion beyond a recognition that physical process is subtle and—so many of us thought—supple in its character. It is attractive to believe that here lies the clue to the way in which we ourselves are able to exercise agency in a top-down manner, as persons executing our intentions. If we play a part in bringing about the future in this holistic fashion, it seems highly reasonable to believe that the Creator does so providentially in some analogous way. What was important about this long discussion, considered from a Christian point of view, was that it drew the science-religion dialogue into closer contact with concerns of central theological significance, a move that I personally very much welcomed. Another development in the Christian camp, taking place in the last few years, has carried this process further, for issues of eschatology have come onto the agenda. In terms of its purely "horizontal" perspective, science prophesies a dismal end for the universe, culminating either in cosmic collapse or in decay. Of course, this predicted futility lies many billions of years in the future, but that surely does not deprive it of significance for theology, since religion, in it comprehensiveness, has to take the longest possible view. In doing so, it also has access to resources unavailable to science, for it can appeal to the "vertical" perspective of the everlasting faithfulness of the Creator. Here, in my view, is the sole source of hope for redemption from futility. Exploration of these eschatological issues is mainly based upon religious insight, but, in assessing the credibility of the concept of a destiny beyond death—either for individuals or for the universe itself—there are some constraints arising from science, not least from its strong suggestion that human beings are to be thought of as psychosomatic unities and not as apprentice angels. Once again, I do not want to try to go into any detail here,[2] but I simply mention this development as an illustration of the vigor and interest characteristic of the contemporary dialogue taking place between science and religion.

What then are my hopes for the future of the dialogue between science and religion? One issue I believe will be at the top of the agenda in the years ahead is the need for a richness of cultural variety and a multiplicity of perspectives. There is a very significant and perplexing difference between science and religion that I did not refer to in my opening remarks. It lies in the universal character of the one and the largely regional character of the other. Of course, modern science arose in particular historical and geographical contexts, but now scientific insight, and scientific techniques for the pursuit of well-motivated belief, have spread worldwide. Stop people in the street in London or Kyoto, Jerusalem, Delhi, or Islamabad, and ask them what matter is made of and—provided you have selected suitably well-informed persons—they will tell you "quarks and gluons." Stop people in the street in those same five cities and ask them a religious question, such as about the nature of ultimate Reality, and the chances are very high that you will receive five very different-seeming answers. I have to say that, as a scientist, I find it worrying, and even to some degree unnerving, that there is this apparently divergent multiplicity of testimony among the world faith traditions. You cannot help wondering at times if the critics might not be right after all, and that religion is really no more than culturally influenced opinion. Since I have already affirmed that I believe that religion is as much concerned with truth as science is, you will realize that I do not give in to this temptation to embrace religious relativism, but I am not altogether sure how to deal effectively and scrupulously with these problems.

One of the reasons that these interfaith issues press upon us inescapably today is that, though the traditions remain strongest in, and centered on, their historic heartlands, there is now a substantial religious diaspora from each tradition spread throughout the world. People of other faiths are no longer odd people in faraway countries, who hold strange beliefs, but some of them are neighbors living down the street. We cannot avoid seeing the integrity of their spiritual lives, and it is no longer possible for us to dismiss them with the thought that they are totally mistaken and we are totally right.

In a broad sense, all the faith traditions are speaking about the same area of human experience, and spiritual dimension of human life and our encounter with the reality of the Sacred. Yet the traditions seem to say such very different things about the character of this human experience and the way in which it should be understood. I find these cognitive clashes extremely puzzling. Of course, cultural factors enter in and refract the different perspectives, but I do not find it possible to attribute all the differences to these effects. The disagreements seem to me to be too great. Is the nature of reality constituted by a clear separation between the Creator and the creation, or is it a monistic unity at its deepest level? Is the human person of enduring and unique significance, or recycled through reincarnation, or ultimately an illusion from which to seek release? Is time a linear path to be trodden or a samsaric wheel from which to seek liberation? It does not seem to me to be at all conceivable that all these answers are equally true.

I am sure that I have things of great importance to learn from my brothers and sisters in other faith traditions, but I think that we can only meet with integrity if I hold to my nonnegotiable Christian beliefs, just as they hold to the particulars of their own tradition. This makes our encounter painful and difficult, but I do not think it can properly occur on any other basis. The attempt to construct a "common denominator" religiosity seems to me to result in an account so bland and anemic that it would not be recognized as adequate by any adherents of a faith tradition, or thought worthy of being taken seriously by them.

I believe that the ecumenical meeting of the world faith traditions will be of prime importance throughout the whole of the third millennium. It will certainly not be easy, but it must be undertaken. The initial ground on which the traditions first meet must not be too threatening. If the conversation starts with questioning each tradition's central tenets, it seems to me that defenses will immediately go up on all sides, which will make the encounter abortive. Yet the meeting must concern issues that are sufficiently serious and important to warrant enduring painful encounter to discuss them. It seems to me that one meeting ground of this kind could be provided by mutual exploration of how the faiths each relate to science and to its understanding of the nature and history of the world in which we live.

Another central task for members of all faiths is to keep abreast of important new scientific developments and to assess their significance for religious understanding. We all have a real responsibility here, not least with respect to the members of our own faith communities, where we need to encourage them not to be suspicious or fearful of the discoveries of science, but to welcome them as further contributions in the great human quest for truth.

Among my hopes for scientific developments in the twenty-first century is the expectation that there will be very important new insights stemming from the study of complex systems. Work on the nonequilibrium thermodynamics of dissipative systems, and the studies of the behavior of computer simulations, undertaken by the complexity theorists, have both revealed the existence of astonishing natural powers for the spontaneous generation of large-scale order. At present these matters are at what one might call the natural-history stage of the investigation of particular instances. Yet surely there must be a deep general theory that underlies these remarkable behaviors. When that is discovered, as I am sure it will be, I anticipate that a consequence will be that *information* (meaning by that, something like the specification of complex dynamical pattern) will take its place alongside that of energy as a basic category for thinking about physical process.

The systems, whose behavior scientists are presently able to discuss in some detail, are of trivial complexity when compared to that of the simplest living cell, let alone to that of the human brain. Yet it seems to me that, if developments take the course that I expect, at least our imaginations will have been enhanced in a potentially very fruitful direction. I have even been bold enough to suggest, in relation to human psychosomatic unity, that we should think of the soul as being the almost infinitely complex information-bearing pattern carried by the matter of the body.

Another science from which we may hope for important future discoveries is neuroscience. At present, as I understand it, much effort, as one might expect, is concentrated on the detailed level of investigations into such particular matters as the neural pathways by which the brain processes visual information. It will be when the subject attains the ability to reach agreed understanding of how to discuss higher levels of integration, moving in the direction of an overarching account of brain functioning, that we may anticipate important interaction taking place with religious thinking. I know, of course, that work has already been done with that aim in mind, but I think that religion has to be somewhat careful about placing too much reliance on scientific insight until the scientists themselves are able to give a fairly unanimous account of what should be said from their point of view.

Will that kind of agreed understanding ever be possible in relation to consciousness studies? Is this, as some would assert, the "last frontier" that scientists will soon begin to cross? Or is consciousness so constitutive of what we are as human beings that we shall never be able to step out of ourselves to gain an objective account of its origin and nature? I do not know the answer, and I think the only way to find out is to see how far we can go with the inquiry. It does seem to me, however, that the prospects are very distant. There seems to be a yawning gap between talk of neural networks and synaptic discharges, however valuable and interesting such talk undoubtedly is, and the simplest mental experience of seeing red and feeling hungry, a chasm that at present we have not the slightest idea how to bridge. In other words, I take the problem of qualia very seriously, as I also do the hard problem of awareness, and I am not at all disposed to accept grandiose claims that consciousness is explained (contra Dennett).

Much work lies ahead, involving, as it must, fruitful contacts and exchanges between all the faith traditions. The resulting dialogue will be global in scope. The task will be hard work, and painful at times as cherished attitudes are subjected to challenge and careful scrutiny. Yet the work will be sustained by a shared desire for truthful understanding, involving as it does those two great sources of insight, science and religion, whose roles are of such fundamental importance and significance for humanity. The International Society for Science and Religion will certainly seek to play its part in this great truth-seeking endeavor.

Notes

1. E. P. Wigner, "The Unreasonable Effectiveness of Mathematics in the Natural Sciences." *Communications on Pure and Applied Mathematics* 13 (1960): 1–14.
2. See J. C. Polkinghorne, *The God of Hope and Its End of the World* (New Haven: Yale University Press/London: SPCK, 2002).

5

Science, Religion, and Culture

FRASER WATTS

THIS IS A TIME when there is growing and understandable concern about the peace and stability of the world order. There is increasing division among different faith traditions, and apprehension about the consequences of those divisions is growing. Tensions are particularly strong within the Abrahamic religions. In the Second World War, relations between those of Christian and Jewish origin descended to an appalling level of inhumanity. Tensions continue between Muslims and Jews surrounding the modern state of Israel. In recent years, the tension between Islam and the Christian West has become increasingly prominent. Religion seems so closely associated with national, racial, and cultural identity that it tends to be a source of tension and instability in the world, however much its teachings might suggest otherwise.

In contrast, science is the most genuinely international movement in the world, and therefore has the potential to be a force for peace and stability. It is also a supreme achievement of human rationality. So, at first blush, it seems that, if each religious tradition could engage more deeply with science, and take on some of its calm, tolerant, rational spirit, there might be an easing of the tensions that arise between different faith traditions.

This statement leads to the two propositions that I propose to consider. The first is that science is objective, rational, and genuinely international. The second is that religion is linked to particular cultures and inherently divisive. There is obviously much plausibility in these propositions. But things are not quite so simple, and one must consider these claims about both science and religion more closely before addressing implications for the dialogue between science and religion.

Science

Science is probably not as culturally neutral and value free as is sometimes supposed and claimed. Contemporary science is dominated by the United States and other Western countries. That alone is enough to ensure that science is not always *perceived* as culturally neutral. But more is at stake here than global politics.

The assumptions of the religious traditions have helped to give rise to science. An assumption of religion is that the world is orderly and lawful, reflecting its Creator, and so amenable to systematic investigation. There is also an assumption that the world is contingent and reflects the absolute free will of its Creator. These two assumptions, lawfulness and contingency, make science likely to be fruitful.

However, different faith traditions have given rise to scientific advance in different periods. For example, in the early part of the second millennium, Islam was particularly important in facilitating scientific advance. However, the current wave of Western-dominated science has arisen in a Christian culture, and no doubt reflects that position in many of its assumptions. There has recently been increasing recognition among intellectual historians of the extent to which apparently secular patterns of thought, including those of science, incorporate counterparts of religious assumptions. For example, the idea of original sin has cropped up again in secular form both in Freud's Id and in the selfish gene of sociobiology. Science in its current Western phase may therefore not be quite as religiously neutral as at first appears.

Science has also arisen out of what is sometimes called "modernity." Modernity is often seen as going back to the early modernity of the seventeenth century, and has continued in a slightly different form in the more secular post-Darwinian world of late modernity. A key feature of modernity has been the search for objectivity, for a neutral, value-free vantage point that shakes off all particular cultural contexts. If it is truly objective in that sense, science should be invariant and unchanging. On that assumption, Third-World science should be no different from American science; there should be no difference, for example, between the science of Islamic and Christian countries.

However, philosophers of science, like historians of science, have become skeptical of these claims to scientific objectivity. Indeed, philosophers have become skeptical about the very idea of being free of any particular vantage point. As Thomas Nagel famously put it, there is no "view from nowhere."[1] Background assumptions always creep in. Let me briefly mention two examples of how that works.

First, science often proceeds by models and analogies. How we understand the world depends on the analogies we have at hand. Science gives rise to technological innovations, which in turn provide models that are used in further scientific inquiry. For example, clockwork mechanisms were important as models in early modern science, and the world was seen as a mechanism. Similarly, computers are important in contemporary science.

Second, science is driven by the needs of the wider society. Notoriously, warfare drives scientific advance, channeling it in certain directions. If the world had been peaceful in the twentieth century, science would almost certainly have proceeded differently. Scientific advance reflects the preoccupations of society, and in particular reflects where society decides to spend its resources.

Sometimes, these kinds of points about science are pushed too far, or further at least than I would want to go. I continue to believe that science is a great achievement of human rationality. I would accept that the rationality of science is not a matter of cold logic, but of human judgment. I would also accept that science can be distorted by nonrational factors, such as the career-building needs of individual scientists. However, I still believe that science remains a paradigm of human rationality.

I also continue to believe that there is scientific progress, despite much controversy about this. True, this progress is not inexorable, and what may look like secure findings at one point in time may need to be rethought in the context of future paradigm shifts. It may also be true that we will never reach the end-point of scientific advance; or, if we did, we would not know it. Nevertheless, clearly there is progress in science, of a kind. We know more now than we used to.

However, science has perhaps been unnecessarily narrow in its approach. In no way do I want to set aside the struggle for objectivity that has been so fruitful, even if that objectivity has not been as complete as is sometimes claimed. However, I believe that there could usefully be some broadening of science, in both method and theory. Science has been the child of the search for objective truth associated with modernity in the West, but it has also been in some ways limited and constrained by the aspiration to value-free objectivity associated with modernity.

Methodologically, I would like to see the human element in science receive greater recognition. There should be more respect for what an imaginative enterprise science is. Scientific enterprise can never be purely mechanical; it depends on human judgment and imagination. Also, too little attention has been given to how scientific discoveries are made, as opposed to how they are demonstrated. What is said about scientific method tends to focus too exclusively on verification and ignores how discoveries are made. I would like to see a broader and more human understanding of how science proceeds.

Theoretically, I would like to see an emancipation of the range of entities and processes that science is prepared to postulate. Physical science has already moved a long way, from assuming that all scientific explanations need to be framed in terms of microparticles, to postulating fields and forces, and then on to the strange world of quantum mechanics. Another broadening that is urgently needed is to give proper weight to top-down explanations in biology, alongside bottom-up explanations. Science needs to move beyond the reductionist mind-set that, if pushed too far, becomes inhuman and distasteful.

It will also be important to have a humble view of science. My own intuition is that we are at present merely at the foothills of scientific inquiry, and that the scientific worldview in a few centuries time will be radically different from our own. The fact that we lack an agreed way of putting together general relativity theory and quantum mechanics is one pointer to that: the lack of any viable neural theory of consciousness is another.

Further emancipation of science is thus needed, both methodologically and theoretically. Such emancipated science will facilitate scientific progress, but I believe that it will also lead to a more humane science that will be more congenial to the world faith traditions. The science we have now, though international in one sense, reflects too much the background assumptions of Western modernity. The science that I hope to see develop will be more genuinely international, because it will transcend those local background assumptions.

We need a more hermeneutic understanding of science. The first step toward hermeneutic sophistication is to recognize that the there is no "view from nowhere" and that what we imagine was purely objective is actually quite context dependent. Having recognized that, there are two appropriate responses. One is to acknowledge the influence of background assumptions and to be quite explicit and specific about how all human rationality, including science, reflects particular sets of assumptions. The other is to use our awareness of how cultural context shapes all human enterprises, including science, to transcend those limitations as far as possible, while still recognizing that we can never move completely beyond those limitations. That will give us a more genuinely international science.

Religion

What of the apparently divisive impact of religion on the world order? The present impact of religion in the world belies the idea that the world is becoming more secular. Secularization may be occurring in parts of Europe, but they are the exception not the rule. Most of the world remains deeply religious.

Important differences exist between so-called religions. Indeed, it may be misleading to talk about "religions" at all. It is not just that the faith traditions of the world differ from one another in important ways; they are not even the same kind of thing. Most religions are concerned, to some degree, with both faith and practice. However, the balance of emphasis between the two differs from one faith tradition to another. For example, Christianity is probably more concerned with truth than Judaism, but less concerned with practice. Such differences affect the importance attached to the dialogue with science in different faith traditions.

Also, some faith traditions are more elective than others, in the sense that people choose to join them or leave them, as they do with Christianity and Western Buddhism, for example. Others are more intertwined with cultural identity. To ask a Hindu or a Jew what is his "religion" is a strange question. Such faith traditions are a matter of cultural identity as much as they are a matter of private experience, morality, and salvation. It is too easy to assume that all religions are counterparts of Western Christianity, whereas in many ways Christianity is the exception among the faith traditions of the world.

Admittedly, in many places in the world Christianity is as much intertwined with cultural identity as any religion could be, and where this happens it is often a particular Christian denomination that becomes a badge of identity. Thus, in Bosnia, cultural groupings are divided religiously into Orthodox Christians, Catholic Christians, and Muslims. In Ireland, the division is between Catholics and Protestants. However, partly because Christianity has given rise to a greater degree of secularization than any other religion, it has also often become more detached from cultural identity than any other faith tradition.

Clearly the teachings of the world's religions have common elements, but that does not mean that all religions are fundamentally the same. Nor should they be. It would be a mistake to try to imitate in religion the objectivity and internationalism associated with science. People adhere to religious traditions in part because they are *their* religions, not someone else's. There would probably be no more enthusiasm for a neutral world religion than there is for speaking Esperanto.

Certainly, religions arise from, and give expression to, cultural identity. But at their best, I believe that they help people to transcend their cultural identity, and to reach out to those beyond their own faith traditions. At their best, religions help the body of humanity to move beyond cultural specificity. There is a kind of "emergentism" here. Religions emerge from particular cultures, but having emerged they often help people to transcend those cultures.

As one example, we could take the teaching of Jesus, who is widely revered as a prophet in many of the world's faith traditions, certainly among all the Abrahamic faiths. The Jewish people had a strong tradition of neighborliness to their own people, but Jesus challenged them to extend their concept of neighborliness to non-Jews, including Samaritans. The Jewish people also had a strong sense of being a chosen people, but Jesus taught them that God's salvation was now for Samaritans and others, not only for themselves. They are lessons that Christians have been slow to learn, and Christians have often seen the church as a new kind of chosen people. I suspect that Jesus would say to the Christian church, as he said to his own people, that they should look beyond their own community.

We increasingly need a distinction between healthy and unhealthy forms of religion that cuts across the distinction between different faith traditions. In some ways, the form of a person's adherence to his or her religion may be more important than to which faith tradition he or she belongs. Unhealthy religion has both social and cognitive features. Socially, unhealthy religion is exclusive, with in-groups and out-groups; it provides a support to people's sense of social identity, but at the cost of engendering hostility to those who do not share that identity. Cognitively, unhealthy religion is closed and dogmatic in its thought forms, and is unable to take different perspectives and viewpoints into account in an integrative way.

I am not arguing here for abandoning particular religious traditions. That would be both futile and inappropriate. However, I am pleading that each faith tradition should be open and flexible, both socially and cognitively. When any faith tradition operates in a healthy way, it helps people to rise above their particular cultural background. Religions that are operating healthily will also find it easier to engage with science. That kind of healthy religion can be achieved while people remain deeply rooted in their own particular faith tradition.

Here, science may help. Though the objectivity of science can be exaggerated, it remains one of the greatest achievements of humanity. It is a moral and spiritual achievement, as much as a technological or theoretical one. It is one of the pinnacles of humanity's search for truth, humility, open-mindedness, and tolerance. The spiritual achievement of humanity that science represents now poses a challenge to the world's religions. The challenge is whether, without abandoning their distinct identities, they can embrace a comparable search for truth, humility, open-mindedness and tolerance.

Relating Science and Religion

A fruitful and harmonious relationship between science and religion needs to be based on recognizing the distinctness of each. Religion cannot pretend to be science, and science should not be treated as a religion. Nevertheless, as we have seen, the differences between science and religion are not always as clear-cut as might at first be imagined.

A fruitful dialogue between science and religion also needs to be based on a humble view of both. The grandiose view of science associated with logical positivism has been progressively abandoned by philosophers of science. It is now agreed that there are no raw facts, and that everything is selected and interpreted within a theoretical context. It is also recognized that there is no linear, inexorable progress in science, but a complex historical development including paradigm shifts. There is agreement, too, that there is no dependable logic by which scientific conclusions are reached but, as Karl Popper put it, a series of "conjectures and refutations."[2]

Religion also has a tendency to be grandiose and arrogant, and to claim absolute truth. However, religion is at its best, and most true to itself, when it is humble. Religious truth takes us into the realm of mystery where we need to tread softly out of respect for the spiritual realm we are approaching. It is arrogant for humans to imagine that they can grasp spiritual truths completely. Also, when approached with arrogance, religion does no practical good. It no longer provides people with the space they need to move and grow toward divine truth and fulfillment. Instead, their religion makes them closed and stunted.

So far, the exploration of the relationship between science and religion has been pursued most vigorously in the context of Christianity. However, those who have approached it within that context have much to learn from people of other faith traditions. As I have indicated at various points in this chapter, there are subtle reasons that the dialogue between science and religion should have developed most vigorously within Christianity, and it is likely that the dialogue will never seem such a high priority to other faith traditions. In part that is because they have other priorities that are not fully shared by Christianity.

Nevertheless, there are good reasons for hoping that the dialogue between science and religion will increasingly become a multifaith one. That will be of great benefit and interest to those currently approaching the dialogue from within Christianity. Also, the dialogue will tend to enrich each faith tradition that engages in it. I care deeply about the dialogue between science and religion, partly because I hope it will lead to a less arrogant, more religiously sympathetic science, but also because I hope that science can help religion to become more open and humble.

Notes

1. Thomas Nagel, *The View From Nowhere* (New York: Oxford University Press, 1986).
2. Karl Popper, *Conjectures and Refutations: The Growth of Scientific Knowledge* (London: Routledge and Kegan Paul, 1963).

6

The State of the International Religion-Science Discussion Today*

PHILIP CLAYTON

THE LATE 1980S AND EARLY 1990S saw an explosion of the global dialogue on science and religion. Both within and across specific religious traditions, scientists and religious believers engaged in a more sustained, more rigorous, and more productive dialogue than at perhaps any earlier point in history. This "internationalizing" of the science-religion dialogue opened in a mood of great optimism. Scientists and religious scholars in many of the world's religions began simultaneously to explore the intersections between modern science and their own religious traditions. In the initial meetings of Muslim, Jewish, and Christian scientists, one experienced a clear sense of being involved in a common project, a sense of commonality that one does not always feel when involved in interreligious dialogues. The mutual respect with which participants viewed one another as fellow scientists certainly contributed significantly to these early successes in the international science-religion dialogue. One could tell that those who were geniuses at drawing lines of connection, such as Professor Seyyed Hossein Nasr, were simultaneously recognized by those in other traditions as pioneers and partners in a common field.

As I pen these words, however, we face a much darker time. No man is an island; what occurs between our politicians and our nations will also affect the discussions between our scientists and our scholars of religion. Unnecessary and ill-conceived wars are being fought, and our hearts are wrenched daily by pictures of the deaths of innocent people. Undoubtedly, wrongs are being committed on both sides, and a balanced discussion of the political situation would have to present it in all its ambiguities. Still, among the wrongs to be acknowledged are the aggressive policies and cultural insensitivity of the current American administration. Saddest of all, one recognizes that some of the misguided policies stem, at least in part, from a wrongly politicized interpretation of Christianity in its relationship to Islamic cultures and nations.

It is not my place to resolve the political questions and to make ultimate assignments of blame or praise. But one does have to be realistic about how the present situation has affected the internationalization of the science-religion dialogue. Clearly, for many Muslims the recent hostilities have done great damage to the partnership in which we were engaged together until only recently. A few years ago leading Muslim scholars happily invited American scholars to international meetings that they were organizing in Pakistan, Indonesia, Morocco, and Iran. Today, that is difficult, if not impossible. One needs only to imagine the American professor standing at the podium before a Muslim audience. Sadly, however much the organizers may respect the American speaker as a person and a scholar, they know that in his language and in the culture that he brings the audience will inevitably see the policies of his government. This fact means that the international science and religion discussion is in the greatest possible crisis that it could be, for when we can no longer meet in each other's countries for lectures and collaborations, we are cut off from one another, and the dialogue is at an end.

I open on this dark note because it is the situation that we currently face. No one should see naive optimism in the proposal that follows. To the contrary, I fear that it will take years to undo the damage that has been done in recent years. But we must not accept defeat; the more difficult the situation in our field becomes, the harder we must work to attempt to reestablish common ground. First we seek, for the sake of science, to reestablish collaborations between our scientists. Then we seek to build upon that scientific exchange, once again involving our religious scholars in science-religion discussions. We know from the brief successes of the past how powerful these discussions can be in overcoming misunderstanding and animosity within our religious communities. And finally, we seek to expand that discussion outward, so as to influence our broader culture in the hope, perhaps, of influencing our leaders and our politicians in the direction of peace and justice.

But what kinds of collaborative programs can possibly have these positive effects in today's climate? In the few pages that remain I wish to describe a program that recently brought together scientists from a variety of religious traditions and allowed them to engage in productive dialogue concerning themes in science and religion. I shall then suggest corrections and supplements to this program that would increase its effectiveness in the present context. Finally, I argue that it is of the highest importance that we work to reestablish and carry out programs of this sort so that we can again bring light into the darkness that currently surrounds us.

Science and the Spiritual Quest

By most measures, Science and Spiritual Quest (SSQ) was a successful program. Between 1995 and 2003 SSQ held sixteen private three-day workshops on two continents, involving 123 new scientists in constructive dialogue at the intersections of science and spirituality. The program also organized seventeen public events in nine countries on four continents. Taken together, these events reached close to twelve thousand audience members firsthand and many millions more through the media—some 250 million, according to the official estimates of one media research firm. Six books covering the research output of SSQ have been published or are currently in production on four different continents. The group's Web site, www.ssq.net, lists four full-length video products and contains a massive amount of supplementary material; further excerpts from the SSQ program are available through the Counterbalance Foundation, www.counterbalance.org. In all, forty-eight different organizations, institutions, and financial supporters became allies in achieving these results.

Could the SSQ program serve as a model for future international collaborations? To answer this question, we must first consider not only what made the SSQ program so successful but also what its limitations and drawbacks were. Only then can we determine ways to adapt and improve this model for the present context.

Chosen were SSQ scientists who could be effective spokespersons for their religious traditions, as well as strong representatives for science. Scientists such as Mehdi Golshani in Tehran earned a hearing as religious persons because of the high respect in which they were held as scientists. Alongside senior figures with international reputations, the program also included other scientists who were younger and less experienced, since their early efforts at connecting their scientific and religious lives brought freshness and authenticity to the dialogue.

It is crucial to consider the format of the private workshops, since that is the feature that, I shall argue, is most worthy of repeating today. The SSQ scientists were divided into groups according to disciplinary interests, and each group met twice, each time in private sessions that lasted for two days. Crucial for the success of these meetings were the in-depth and sometimes personal interviews that were conducted with each scientist prior to the meeting. Each scientist was asked to describe how he personally experienced the "double identity" of being a scientist and a religious believer—not only where the two sides of his identity enhanced each other but also where he experienced difficulties. These interviews were transcribed and were distributed in advance to the other participants. Thus, when they met for the first time, they already shared the sort of intimacy and trust that comes from honest introspection and self-disclosure.

In one sense, what occurred at the private workshops was not extraordinary. Each scientist had an hour to summarize his understanding of science from his religious perspective. Two other scientists, usually from two other religious traditions, then raised questions and made comments about what they had heard, and the entire group engaged in discussion with the speaker. The results of the process were extraordinary. Because of the personal nature of the comments and the insight they represented, each participant recognized that the struggles and the moments of integration described by the speaker were not dissimilar to his own. In no way were the differences between the religious traditions obscured. Still, while recognizing these differences one also came to see deep underlying connections in each person's struggle to integrate his religious belief with contemporary science.

The second meeting occurred six months later and offered the opportunity to move from the personal to the conceptual level. In preparation for this meeting, each scientist prepared a careful position statement. These papers, which were circulated to the other participants in advance, showed where contemporary science could be integrated with the author's tradition, where the common understanding of science might need to be modified, and where changes in the usual interpretation of his particular religious tradition might be necessary. At the actual workshop, the words of the presenters and commentators again led to intense exploratory discussions of the topics. And once again the scientists became allies to each other as each one attempted to find a more powerful and effective way to state his own position.

Many of the scientists were then invited to present their position papers at public forums around the world. In all, seventeen public events were held in nine countries on four continents. Not only scientists but also religious leaders and interested laypersons were invited to hear the presentations and to engage in sustained discussion with the speakers. Newspaper and journal articles about the meeting appeared in many different languages around the world, and many of the presentations were collected into books that were later published. In this way, the sort of common understanding that can only be achieved in small groups of experts—thanks to extended discussions, careful listening, and a deep level of trust—was subsequently made available to a much larger audience, spreading the impact of the program far beyond the circle of participating scientists.

Program for the Future

There were, of course, weaknesses in the particular details of the SSQ program. The program leaders were all Christians, and the center that administered the program had a particular interest in Christian theology. Some of the selections of participating scientists were arbitrary, since the selection committee was simply unaware of scientists who would have been ideal participants. Although the public events took place around the world, the workshops themselves were all held in the West. Not enough of the participants were invited to speak at the public conferences, so that not all of the ideas were heard in public. Sadly, too few of the conferences took place within the Islamic world.

One wants to know, therefore, what would be the ideal form for the religion-science discussion to take in the future, so that it could be as effective and influential as possible? In what ways might the SSQ program, in a corrected and improved form, serve as a model? Rather than dwelling on the past, we must hunt for the most fruitful opportunities for the future. To make the question manageable, let's limit the discussion to possible programs involving Muslim, Jewish, and Christian scientists only.

One imagines, first of all, a consortium of at least three centers, one drawn from each of the three religious traditions. Leadership and administration of the joint science and religion project would be shared equally between the three, with each playing some role in hosting and supporting the program. Most important, decisions concerning participating scientists would be made jointly by the leaders of the three institutes. After all, it is not easy to find scientists who are both representative of their religious traditions and also willing and able to engage in open, exploratory dialogue with members of other traditions.

The workshops themselves, and of course the final conferences, would be divided equally between locations that are primarily Muslim, Jewish, and Christian. Each workshop group would consist of fifteen scientists—five from each religious community—who share a common area of scientific work. The task of moderating at each of the individual workshops could be shared among the leadership staff, with representatives of at least two of the traditions sharing the role of chair at any given time.

It is not hard to imagine what would be the positive effects of carrying out this truly international project on "Science and the Spiritual Quest in the Abrahamic Traditions." Indeed, in today's context the mere existence of a cooperative program of this sort would be a powerful statement, even before any concrete results were achieved. The relationships built among the participating scientists themselves would be transformative: there is nothing like the experience of internalizing the perspective of another person, understanding it both in its similarities to and in its differences from one's own perspective. The mutual understanding that occurs through discussions of the interviews and through cooperative work on the various position papers would itself be worth the effort of running the program.

But it is through the organization of the public events that the broadest and clearest impact would be felt. These large-scale meetings would be events of great significance both for the international scientific committee and for our respective religious communities. In today's context, one can be sure that the international media would flock to report on them. In fact, the appearance of leading Muslim, Jewish, and Christian scientists on the same platform would be such a charged event that one has to worry about whether it will be possible to find safe venues where the events can take place. One wonders, for example, whether Muslim scientists would feel safe appearing on a public stage at any major university in Israel today, and one can imagine the difficulties of hosting Jewish and Christian scientists at certain locations in the Islamic world. Some compromises would certainly be necessary. Thus, for example, the SSQ meeting on "The Three Monotheisms" was held in southern Spain—which has long been a meeting ground for scholars from the three Abrahamic traditions—rather than in Tel Aviv as originally planned.

Why Should One Attempt Interreligious Discussion?

In the end, the motivation for pursuing interreligious science-religion discussions must come from within each individual religious tradition. Leading Muslim scholars have shown convincingly that is ample reason within the Qur'an and within the Islamic intellectual traditions for a close dialogue between contemporary science and Muslim thought and practice. The same is true, though for different reasons, for Judaism and Christianity. But one wants to know: is there also a Muslim motivation for an ongoing dialogue between the various religious traditions on this topic? This is a question that I am not competent to answer.

It might be helpful, however, to pause to review some of the motivations that a Christian scholar might have for engaging in an interreligious conversation on science and religion. In the Protestant Christian tradition, the task of interpreting the scriptures and the history of the church—not to mention the history of the world as a whole—is placed upon each individual. If God is the God of the whole cosmos and of all of history, then everything in the world, and all parts of history, are relevant to our efforts to discern the divine will and action. For most Christians, and certainly for liberal Protestants like myself, God's revelation is not limited to the Christian tradition alone. Over the last three hundred years Protestants have struggled to understand how to be faithful to their own tradition while at the same time acknowledging that divine revelation goes beyond any neat set of categories we may have developed. The concept of revelation is two-sided: there must be a speaking or broadcasting by God, and there must be a receiving and comprehending of the revelation by human agents. If this is true, then all factors that are relevant to humanity's comprehension of the world and its Creator—including the full complexity of our scientific, cross-cultural, and interreligious understanding—will be relevant to the project of interpreting the divine will.

This means that we have much to gain from a multireligious approach to the science and religion discussion. By ourselves we may see only one side of the whole picture. But when we learn to listen to those of other traditions—and especially to those who share our belief in the same self-revealing God and who trace their lineage back to the same Father Abraham—we are enriched in our understanding of God and God's relationship to the sciences of the natural world.

I believe that Christians should acknowledge another reason that makes an interreligious approach to the religion-science field particularly important to us. For much of its history, Christianity has tragically allowed itself to be associated with absolutist claims, claims that have sometimes manifested themselves in imperialist, colonialist, and warlike actions. Just when we think that the last of these tendencies has been eradicated from the Christian world, one is disturbed and disappointed to find that the tendencies are not gone after all. This is why it is particularly important for Christians to engage in ongoing dialogue with representatives of other religious traditions: when we do so, we can see much more clearly what is peaceful and positive about our tradition, and what dangerous potentials we must continue to avoid. When Christians listen carefully to what those in other religions are saying to us, their words serve as a sort of mirror, which provides greater self-understanding and helps ward off misapplications of our tradition.

Conclusion

I have described an interreligious project in the field of science and religion, to be called Science and the Spiritual Quest in the Abrahamic Traditions (SSQAT). Outlining the strengths of the Science and the Spiritual Quest program (1995–2003) and admitting its weaknesses and inadequacies, I argued that SSQAT offers a model for future work in the field that is both productive and urgently required. Further, I described some of the motivations that Christians might have for engaging in such a collaborative program.

The reasons for and against supporting such a program will clearly be different for Muslims. My hope is that the concrete proposals and reasons offered here will call forth responses from Islamic scholars, who alone are in the position to say whether there are Islamic reasons for cooperative interreligious projects of this sort. If they do indeed find religious motivations of their own to pursue a project like this, together we can then explore what theoretical foundations there are for future science-religion programs and what types of programs would be of most interest to Muslim scientists and to scholars of Islam. And may God bless the outcome of our work!

*This chapter originally appeared in the *Journal of Islam and Science* 2, no. 1 (Summer 2004), reprinted with permission by the publisher.

Part 3
Perspectives from World Faith Traditions

7

Judaism and Science

A CONTEMPORARY APPRAISAL

CARL FEIT

JUDAISM IS A FAIRLY ANCIENT RELIGION, tracing its roots back approximately three thousand years. This long history has placed it in contact with many of the great civilizations of the world; for example, Greek, Babylonian, Persian, Roman, Christian, and Muslim. The nature of this contact has varied from the most cordial to the most hostile of relationships; nevertheless in each case significant interactions and cross-fertilizations have occurred. Modern science is primarily a product of Western thought. Jews and Judaism have been both participants and observers of its growth and development, and it would take more than a single essay to detail this long and intertwined relationship. Indeed, a vast amount of detailed scholarship has been produced on various aspects of this topic.

A new era in the relationship between science and religion can be marked with the publication of Ian Barbour's *Religion in an Age of Science*. Since its publication there has been a growing interest in both religious and academic circles in exploring new relationships and interactions between religion and science, with an ever-expanding focus on exploring new natural theologies and new theologies of nature.

Most practicing Jews have never seen any inherent conflict between Judaism and science. The general rationale adopted has been that of Moses Maimonides (1135–1204) and many other early scholars who stated that both Torah (revealed wisdom) and science (the study of the "works of God's hands") can never be in conflict and in fact offer complementary approaches to an appreciation of God's wisdom and nature.

I will illustrate this long-standing and consistent tradition within normative Judaism by quoting brief, relevant excerpts from both Maimonides' definitive code of Jewish law, the Mishneh Torah (twelfth century), and from the writings of the greatest twentieth-century spokesman of modern Orthodoxy, Rabbi Joseph B. Soloveitchik.

Maimonides, Mishneh Torah, Fundamentals of the Torah, Chapter 2

1. Everyone is obligated to have love and awe for the awesome, almighty God as it is stated in scriptures: "You shall love the Lord your God with all your heart and soul," and "Have awe of the Lord."

2. And by what method does one achieve this love and awe? When one contemplates His amazing and awesome works and creations, and sees in them His wisdom, of which there is no measure and no end, then there will be awakened in him an intense desire to love, praise, and glorify Him and come to know more about Him, as King David sang, "My soul thirsts for the living, eternal God."

Mishneh Torah, Rules of Repentance, Chapter 10

6. It is well known and obvious that love of God is not firmly rooted in a person's heart, unless he continually strives to develop it with all of his abilities. A person's love of God is commensurate with his knowledge of God, if great then great and if scant then scant. Therefore a person must devote himself to learn and understand the sciences and other branches of knowledge that will give him insight and understanding of his Creator as I have explained above.

The following is an extremely revealing passage taken from *The Emergence of Ethical Man* by Rabbi Joseph B. Soloveitchik.[1] It demonstrates Soloveitchik's understanding of the close affinity between halakhic analysis and scientific methodology.

The Jewish Understanding of Organic Matter

> Let us now analyze the Jewish viewpoint regarding the relationship of man-plant by inspecting the halakhic analysis of things organic.
>
> Organic plant life forms one of the most important regions which Halakha seeks to understand. In other words, the plant is a halakhic cognitive object. A whole order (seder) of the Mishna deals with zer'aim (plants). The method which the Halakha applies in this field is part of the general halakhic methodology:
>
> 1. Halakhic realia; the Halakha aims at factual description and causalistic explanation that is based on observation and induction.
>
> 2. Halakhic apriorism. The Halakha organizes the realia given by observation into halakhic constructs, or a priori schemata, which convert the sensuous data into halakhic-objective order.
>
> In reference to zer'aim, to plants, the Halakha first interprets the realia in a descriptive and explanatory manner and then tries to fit them into a halakhic matrix. As to the interpretation of the realia, the Halakha is extremely objective and scientific. It is concerned with the morphological problem of species and genera. General botanic systematization is a part of the Halakhic interpretation. Such a classification is of the utmost importance. The concepts of "kind" and "species" carry full halakhic validity. The method of systematic description, of abstraction, is similar to that of our general botany and zoology.

Judaism as a religion can largely be understood as living a life in such a way that the moral and religious norms of the Torah are incorporated into daily personal and communal life. As such Judaism is more focused on human conduct rather than a core of beliefs. In order to understand the contemporary dynamics of the relationship between Judaism and science it is necessary to understand certain of the basic structures of traditional Jewish thought. In particular, I would like to explain the essential features of Halakha, or traditional Jewish law, those rules and regulations that are seen as defining what it means to live a Jewish life. I discuss the structure of Jewish law under five headings: written law, oral law, Talmud, Shulkhan Arukh, and Responsa literature.

Written law. Jewish religious law (Halakha) derives originally from biblical texts, primarily those found in the Pentateuch or five books of Moses. These would include the laws embodied in the Ten Commandments, the rules of Sabbath rest, and the dietary code. These laws are traditionally viewed as being divinely mandated and revealed to Moses and the children of Israel at the revelation that took place at Mount Sinai. The rest of the books of the Jewish Bible (or Old Testament) contain much that is important historically and morally, but do not have the same legal weight as the books of Moses.

Oral law. Traditional Judaism also recognizes an ancient oral tradition that consists of explanations, interpretations, and clarifications of biblical law. The oldest of these strata of oral law is ascribed to Moses himself, who is viewed as having incorporated detailed instruction as he taught the written law to the Jewish nation. This process of teaching and explaining was continued by the subsequent leaders of each generation.

Talmud. In the course of time, rabbinic enactments and extensions of biblical law were legislated to deal with changing circumstances and new historical realities. The entire corpus of legal discussion, analysis, and legislation was codified over time. The two most important codifications were the Mishna of Rabbi Judah the Prince (circa 220 C.E.) and the Talmud (circa sixth century C.E.). The Talmud is the magnum opus of Jewish law and incorporates the actual text of the Mishna, submitting it to detailed discussion and extensive analysis of its implications and application.

Shulkhan Arukh. Post-Talmudic Jewish law is found in various codifications of the law which sought to distill the Talmudic discussions into the final conclusion of normative practice. Most notable and authoritative of these codifications is the Shulkhan Arukh (Prepared Table) of Rabbi Yosef Karo compiled in the mid-sixteenth century.

Responsa literature. In addition to the above-described works there has always been and continues to be a tremendous body of literature known as Responsa. Responsa represents the attempts of rabbinic scholars of each generation to apply the principles of Halakha to the ever-changing realia of society and technology. A single responsum is the written response of a particular rabbinic scholar to a specific question posed to him. Responsa are in general very specific and rarely deal with theoretical questions or issues that have no immediate legal ramifications affecting behavior.

With this as background, I think that it is understandable that the ferment in religious/science circles has been far less of a hot item in Jewish circles than it has been in other religions. At the risk of oversimplifying the reality, I would say that Judaism's approach to science in the modern era has been pragmatic rather than theologic. That is to say, since Halakha must confront the realia of daily existence, and scientific innovations have completely revolutionized every aspect of our lives, halakhic scholars have had to keep abreast of scientific development in order to be able to see how they fit into the halakhic world. So while there is a relative paucity of writings on modern theological issues of Judaism and science, there are literally thousands of articles and Responsa dealing with every conceivable practical aspect of science and Halakha. These run from the relatively mundane, such as the permissibility of using electronic devices on the Sabbath, to the most profound and perplexing of issues, such as the permissibility and/or desirability of human stem-cell research and development.

The vast majority of these articles are published in Hebrew, tend to be technical in nature, and are written for internal consumption, that is, other halakhically committed Jews. In the United States and Israel, there are about ten regularly published journals almost completely devoted to issues of medicine/science and its halakhic implications. Some examples of the extent of material that has been produced may be helpful.

Rabbi Moshe Feinstein (d. 1993) was considered to be the greatest interpreter of Jewish law living in the United States during the twentieth century. He replied to questions submitted to him on a daily basis and was often the "court of last resort" for difficult questions. Many of his responses have been published in a multivolume work called the *Igrot Moshe* (Letters of Moshe), which runs six volumes and counting. An unofficial, and cursory, count conducted by myself indicates no fewer than 150 responses dealing with medical and/or scientific issues. Rabbi Eliezer Waldenburg, a great Jerusalem scholar, also produced a multivolume series with hundreds of responses dealing largely with medical issues confronting doctors, patients, and the administration of Shaarey Zedeck Hospital in Jerusalem.

In these responses, Jewish sages apply the principles of Halakha to new, unfolding, and developing technologies. In order to do this they must thoroughly understand the nature of the new technologies and therefore at least have a working knowledge of the scientific principles behind it.

Occasionally, some of this material finds its way into more mainstream literature. Dr. Fred Rosner, director of the Department of Medicine at Queens Hospital Center and professor of medicine at Mount Sinai School of Medicine, has published several summaries of Jewish opinion on medical issues in mainstream medical journals. One very comprehensive example is an article entitled "Jewish Medical Ethics," which appeared in the *Journal of Clinical Ethics* in the fall of 1995. In this article, Rosner introduces and then summarizes Jewish halakhic opinion on topics such as contraception, artificial insemination, in vitro fertilization and screening, abortion, Tay-Sachs and other genetic screening, euthanasia, and abortion. He mentions, though does not analyze in depth, such issues as truth telling and professional secrecy, sterilization, transsexual surgery, sex selection, genetic engineering, human experimentation, suicide, organ donations and transplants, embalming, and cremation.

For traditional practicing Jews, the eternal validity of the Torah and its values are the basic tenets of communal and personal life. Since we live in an era where the world has been transfigured by scientific progress, detailed knowledge of science is a sine qua non for the full application and integration of Torah into daily life. In addition, the scientific study of God's created world offers an optimal approach to enhancing one's love, awe, and reverence for the Creator of the universe.

Note

1. Joseph B. Soloveitchik, *The Emergence of Ethical Man*, ed. Michael S. Berger (Jersey City, N.J.: KTAV Publishing House, Inc., 2005), 17.

8

Is the Science and Religion Discourse Relevant to Islam?

MUNAWAR A. ANEES

The Matrix

The discourse on science and religion has come of age. Of the three Abrahamic traditions, the Jewish and the Christian debate seem to be gaining a sufficient degree of maturity. Here, the epistemological and theological issues are open to question with an extensive body of literature on the subject. Whatever the underpinnings of modernity or the later period, it is not uncommon to find scientist-theologians or believing scientists across the West.

On the contrary, the issue of science and religion in the Muslim context is one of confusion and curiosity. This brief essay sets out to probe if a discourse on science and religion bears any relevance to the Muslim world. It looks at the Islamic concept of knowledge as derived from the Qur'an and the Tradition of the Prophet, its manifestation through the ages, challenges of modernity and postmodernism, and finally, what the future holds for the Muslim discourse.

Knowledge as a Unity

The archetypal concept of *Tawhid* (unity of God) is central to any Muslim discourse on epistemology. Tawhid is a worldview wherefrom emanate all Islamic values. The unflinching faith in this core value lies at the heart of Muslim ethos. Little wonder that Muslim philosophers and theologians have jealously guarded this primal attribute of God in formulating constructs and juridical opinions.

An Islamic understanding of the nature and practice of knowledge (*'ilm*), therefore, must be tied to the concept of Tawhid. At its face value the apparent dichotomy of "science" *and* "religion" would appear to be a fallacy. Islamic epistemology recognizes knowledge only as a unity, a manifestation of God's gift to humankind where He Himself is the ultimate source of all knowledge. The Qur'anic pronouncement makes it clear that God created Adam and taught him what he knew not. He granted him an ascendancy over the angels and made him His vicegerent on Earth. The divine nature and moral nuance of knowledge in the Islamic worldview set the basic premise: all knowledge comes from God and is organically linked as a unifying entity. The human endeavor in knowing is but an act of mercy of God.

The Qur'an is replete with references to knowledge, its attributes, and its different embodiments. It is instructive to note that the first word of the first revelation of the Qur'an was *Iqra*, setting the divine command to *read*. The same prime verses proclaim that it is He Who taught (the use of) the pen and taught man that which he knew not. There are nearly eight hundred verses in the Qur'an that exhort the believers to delve into knowledge. They speak of intellect, wisdom, discernment, and vision as signs of the Creator. Critical observation of Nature is held by the Qur'an as one of the gateways to the knowledge of the Divine.

How pivotal the Qur'anic emphasis is upon knowledge, both divine and natural, is shown by the fact that the Prophet himself is urged to pray to God for an increase in his knowledge. According to several *Ahadith* (Traditions) of the Prophet, he continually reminded Muslims to strive in the path of knowledge. He is known to have said that the pen of the scholar is mightier than the sword of the fighter. He is said to have elevated men of learning to the status of prophets. Even if one needed to travel to China in pursuit of knowledge, one must do, he declared. In the Prophetic Tradition, the acquisition of knowledge is an obligation of every Muslim man and woman just as he counseled them to seek knowledge from cradle to grave.

The Qur'anic and the Prophetic commandments on knowledge provide the matrix within which Islamic epistemology operates. The foregoing references to some of these commandments make it clear that all knowledge is divine in origin, an act of mercy upon humankind. As such, a reductionist approach to knowledge carries little meaning within the Islamic framework. This is not to say that subtleties of reductionism, such as theory reductionism or process reductionism, are ignored.

The point that needs to be highlighted is that Islamic epistemology has a single, divine source of knowledge. Human knowledge is but a manifestation of that knowledge. The "creation" of human knowledge takes place within the divine mold. For utilitarian purposes man is free to resort to a methodology of his choice. But it runs contrary to the essence of Islamic theory of knowledge for man to view any piece of knowledge as his own creation. On the contrary, Islam appeals to man's faculties of reason as an instrument of divine understanding and holds acquisition knowledge as an act of worship.

Knowledge in Action

Imbued with the spirit of Tawhid, early Muslim civilization made phenomenal strides in imbibing and advancing all types of knowledge. Within the first three centuries of the advent of Islam, Muslims became heir to the intellectual traditions of a number of civilizations including Greek, Roman, Persian, and Hindu. They were motivated in their zeal for knowledge by the Qur'anic and the Prophetic commands. How those commands were translated into reality during the formative phase of Muslim history will not fail to impress any impartial observer.

It is not an exaggeration that the medieval Muslim period witnessed one of the finest juxtapositions of spiritual and natural knowledge. For instance, a number of fundamental contributions in astronomy were made because geographically dispersed Muslims wanted to determine the exact direction of *Qibla* in Mecca for performing their five daily prayers. Much the same way the Qur'an provided a great impetus for evolution in other areas of learning, such as health sciences, philosophy, linguistics, and geography.

Similarly, the pioneering efforts in shaping a methodology of transmission of the Prophetic Tradition gave rise to many auxiliary disciplines. The issue of integrity of the received text was deemed crucial for the preservation and transmission of the Tradition. Two things mattered: the transmitters themselves and the text. The methodological rigor applied in fulfilling these two prerequisites for the accuracy of the recorded Tradition gave birth to what we know today as biographical dictionaries. This was an offshoot of *ilm ar-rijal*—the Arabic equivalent of *Who's Who*. Ibn Khallikan's work is one of the classics, as is Ibn an-Nadim's *al-Fihrist*, for being the world's first biobibliography.

Against an injustice of historiography, new literature is emerging to show that Muslims were not mere transmitters of ancient wisdom. They skillfully acquired knowledge of arts and sciences from distant lands and different civilizations. Much of what triggered the European Renaissance can be safely attributed to the stock of knowledge transmitted via the Arabic translations of the ancient texts. Above all, for nearly five hundred years Muslim Spain remained a living witness to the free flowering of intellect where Jews, Christians, and Muslims engaged in the legendary *Convivencia*. Unfortunately, with the Reconquista came the Inquisition, forced conversion, and the expulsion of Jews and Muslims from Spain. This coincided with the rise of the Ottoman Empire where Muslim scholastic tradition received due patronage. However, by the early eighteenth century this tradition began to show signs of degeneration. Future centuries would witness a further deterioration of Muslim intellectual prowess.

Martyrs of Modernity?

For a long time, "Civilization of the Book"—so aptly conveying the Qur'anic essence—remained one of the oft-quoted attributes of Muslim society. By the late nineteenth century, the same civilization presented itself on the lowest rung of the intellectual ladder. Another century would pass, and the same people who upheld intellectual tradition as a religious obligation would engage in book burning in Bradford, England.

On the one hand, a satisfactory explanation for the decay in Muslim intellect remains a challenge for historians and social scientists. On the other hand, a squabble over the chronological sequence of the decline makes no positive contribution to our understanding of the phenomenon. It is without intellectual depth and reduces Muslim scholarship to merely an entry in the annals of history.

Beyond the loss of political power and economic territory, the insular shift in the Muslim attitude toward the Enlightenment can easily be seen as one of the major factors in this transition. Large-scale colonization that coincided with the European Enlightenment left lasting imprints upon Muslim ability to face the challenges of modernity. Even though two centuries of colonization have ended and the classical variety of colonialism has been dismantled, the deep wounds inflicted upon the Muslim psyche make their presence felt.

Colonial powers are not blameless. But to attribute all Muslim ills to the colonial experience is tantamount to escapism, suggesting a reluctance for self-analysis and self-criticism. More than half a century has elapsed since the classical colonialism departed from much of the Muslim world. However, Muslims continue to harp on about the colonial legacy instead of engaging in positive self-reflection.

The omnipresent bogey of colonialism has led to both fear and rejection. At the same time, it is a failure of Muslim perception to take stock of the ideational currents in the West. This failure is highly pronounced in the context of scientific and technological progress, where lack of substantive knowledge remains one of the major obstacles for the growth of a culture of science.

Not long ago the reluctance to accept lithography, condemnation of the telegraph as a toy of the devil, and refusal to acknowledge the human lunar landing were reflective of public understanding of science. Similarly, the ban on artificial insemination by husband in at least one Muslim country shows how well biology is taught and understood for theologians to issue such a verdict. Not discounting the meager support for science education and research in the Muslim world there are serious setbacks in developing positive and critical attitudes toward science and its products. This, in turn, carries deep implications for a healthy engagement of science and religion.

Apologists at Large

The Muslim experience of modernity has produced a healthy crop of apologists who come in all shapes and forms. Perhaps two centuries are not enough to shed the vestiges of nostalgia that Muslims in general carry with them. The power of the West has instilled a fear for which nostalgic indulgence seems to offer a convenient escape route. The most visible and deceptively gratifying approach is to seek "scientific" answers in the Qur'an.

The Qur'anic literalism has mushroomed over the last four or so decades. It all started with the publication of a book by a French medical doctor, Maurice Bucaille, who marshaled the argument that the Qur'anic account of the "scientific" discoveries is far more accurate than that of other holy scriptures. He set the textual criticism in an ontological perspective and tried to argue that the Qur'an foretold what science was discovering today.

Bucaille became an instant celebrity throughout the Muslim world. He seemed to have hit just the right chord in a milieu rife with all shades of apologia: Astronaut Neil Armstrong was rumored to have heard the Muslim call to prayer (*adhan*) as he landed on the Moon. Nobody ever questioned the scientific basis of such an event! On the contrary, at least two Muslim states officially sponsored international conferences to investigate the "scientific miracles" of the Qur'an. A permanent institution is now actively engaged in this line of research.

The literalist approach to the Qur'an covers a vast number of scientific disciplines from embryology to geology. We are now told that the speed of light can be directly calculated from the Qur'an and that one can harvest spiritual energy simply by controlling the spirits (*jinn*). Another pastime is to indulge the "mathematical miracle" of the Qur'an. An Egyptian computer expert, Rashad Khalifah, who later made a claim to prophethood and was murdered under mysterious circumstances in Tucson, Arizona, made lopsided arguments that the figure 19 is the key to understanding the Qur'an. According to Khalifah, scientific discoveries lie hidden in different permutations of the figure 19, and all one needs is a high-speed computer-aided numerological analysis of the Qur'an to unravel that knowledge.

Another celebrity of the apologist hall of fame is Canadian embryologist Keith Moore, whose "scientific" study of the human embryological sequence in the Qur'an has won him a place in some textbooks on the subject. It is true that the Qur'an mentions a certain sequence of human reproduction from conception to full fetal growth. However, one makes such literal interpretations of the sacred text vis-à-vis the biological reality at the risk of intellectual peril. For all measures, biology has both structural and functional levels. It is unclear at what level one can make a safe and valid interpolation.

Qur'anic literalism is a fallacy. The apologetic zeal wants to "prove" the truth of the Qur'an by invoking the scientific methodology. In its second chapter the Qur'an makes a statement of self-truth proclaiming itself to be a book in which there is no doubt. Therefore, it runs contrary to the fundamental premise of Islamic epistemology to argue that the Qur'an is in need of a validation of its truth claim by scientific methods. That makes belief subservient to the human agency, denying the divine role in imparting knowledge. At the same time, it negates the organic unity of all knowledge.

Anyone familiar with the basics of scientific methodology knows that the method is its own nemesis. It is ever changing, with the interpretation always requiring a fresh validation. That makes the scientific methodology bound to a spatiotemporal frame of reference. This procedural flaw does not apply to the sacred text. Its pronouncement has a seal of authenticity and finality, though subject to differing interpretations.

If one is to accept the newly discovered equivalences between the sacred text and the scientific account, then what is one supposed to make of the scared text once the scientific ground shifts and new interpretations are in vogue? The unilateral quest for scientific authentication and validation of the sacred text is totally oblivious of the implications for belief once the results fall short of a self-fulfilling prophecy. Perhaps it is safe to recognize that the phenomenological statements in the sacred text are simply normative in essence and not amenable to transient human perception.

Science à la Islam

The environmental movement in the West is generally credited with the rise of social accountability of science and the end of its heroic image. Among others coming under the influence of these currents, the coinage "Islamic science" entered the modern debate. Seyyed Hossein Nasr is a deserving protagonist of this new mode of thought. His achievement lies in creating a scholastic frame of reference to initiate a discourse on the interfaces between science and Islam. His prolific writings on the subject constitute the groundwork for a modern philosophical and historical interpretation of science in Muslim society. This is a far cry from the nostalgia and apologia that have characterized much of the discourse.

Beyond Nasr's fundamental contribution in giving a face to Islamic science, the subject continues to beg for a definition. A half-baked attempt at "Islamization" of knowledge has shown that by merely putting a prefix to the titles of disciplines—Islamic astronomy, Islamic biology, Islamic economics—no scholarly purpose is served. Taking a cue from the idea that knowledge is not value-free and is generated within the framework of an ideology, Islamization seeks to infuse—nay, rather, reinvent—modern knowledge with a top layer of Islamic values.

A critical look at the Islamization methodology exposes its flaws. It appears to have many similarities with the creation/evolution debate and the uproar over intelligent design. One fails to find answers as to how the Islamic values would be integrated within the body of knowledge, how those same values would affect the processes of knowing, and finally, how this newly packaged knowledge would share its common heritage with knowledge generated outside the Islamic framework?

A few writers, including some neophytes, have attempted to present Islamic science as a panacea for the ills of the Muslim community. Their approach is either to take a cursory look at the history of science in Islam and condemn the Western science for its alleged destruction of the Muslim societies or to transplant a few isolated concepts from the *Shariah* onto the working models of science. Both suffer from intellectual thinness. While one reduces Islamic science to an insular, passive, and xenophobic mode, the other makes a mockery of the genuine Muslim scholarship in shoddy journalistic parlance.

Besides Nasr, perhaps the only positive development is a biannual publication, *Journal of Islamic Science*, published by the Muslim Association for the Advancement of Science, Aligarh, India. For almost two decades the journal has survived against heavy odds. Its utility lies in providing a forum for debate, no matter how small. Moreover, the editors have consistently labored on expounding the Islamic value system without making premature conclusions about Islamic science.

Frightening Future

The Muslim fall from grace is a civilizational issue. The multiple causes for the fall can neither be reduced to classical or neocolonialism nor to someone's political whims. It is self-deceptive to mock the West while making arrogant claims about the absence of dichotomy of knowledge in Islam. In any search for the reasons of the fall, therefore, the issue of science and religion remains highly significant.

The relevance of the science and religion discourse for Islam can easily be discerned through the rise and fall of knowledge across the Muslim historical spectrum. Some comfort may be derived in realizing the organic unity of all knowledge. But that is the point from which emerges a real challenge to the Muslim intellect. To invoke false pride in comparing the status of knowledge with other societies, where modernity or secularism poses its peculiar problems, is a failure of both perception and judgment.

The paradigm of Tawhid as the raison d'être for Islamic epistemology and the Prophetic Tradition are no impediment to knowledge in Islam. On the contrary, they offer a matrix around which free inquiry is not only encouraged but made obligatory as a matter of belief. The task before the Muslim intellectual, therefore, is not to engage in futile debates with the West but to map out a strategy to exploit the unified knowledge.

The confusion about the status of knowledge is one of the critical issues in the science and religion discourse in the Islamic context. Literalism, apologia, Islamization, and the recently vulgarized version of "Islamic science" are but offshoots of an obscurantism that continues to plague the evolution of Muslim intellect. Notwithstanding the economic and political obstacles to the advancement of knowledge in the Muslim world, there is a serious epistemological stagnation caused by an explosive mix of apologia and personal political agendas.

While the religious establishment has not known educational innovation for a long time, the intellectuals are engaged in an imaginary discourse that has little bearing on Islamic theory of knowledge or the socioeconomic utility of knowledge. If the present status quo in Muslim philosophy is any yardstick, then there is an urgent need to initiate a valid and authentic discourse on science and Islam as one of the major intellectual challenges of our times.

9

Science and Hinduism

SOME REFLECTIONS

B. V. SUBBARAYAPPA

INDIA IS A LAND OF MANY RELIGIONS—endogenous as well as exogenous. The major endogenous, or Indic, ones are the orthodox Hinduism and the heterodox Buddhism, Jainism, and Sikhism. The exogenous ones are the Islamic, Christian, and the immigrant Zoroastrianism. The latter ones, however, have had a long history and are an inseparable part of Indian religious tradition. I shall not attempt to discuss this milieu vis-à-vis science in India, but rather confine myself to an overview of Hinduism, and its encounter with modern science.

It is difficult indeed to have a capsuled definition of Hinduism as a religion in the accepted sense of the word. Over the two millennia at least, what is designated as Hinduism has been a blend of faith and the so-called God-realization ritual practices, sublime as well as profane—sublime in their nonmaterial goals, and profane in the performance of rituals for material cravings. Hinduism has its lofty conceptions, ranging from the reality of the knowable world and even beyond on the one hand to, on the other, the illusory or ephemeral nature of the phenomenal world.

THE TRADITION

Hinduism is an intertwined tradition encompassing material life as well as spirituality, worldly involvement as well as detachment. Tradition dies hard in India, and religious/spiritual tradition has been the bedrock, as it were, of the Hindu way of life. From the Ṛgvedic times (ca. 1500 B.C.) to the present, a perceptible facet of Hindu ethos has been the religious inclination of the elite and the laity alike. Its religio-philosophical matrix is a confluence of the triple pathways of (1) human action (*karma mārga*), (2) divine devotion (*bhakti mārga*), and (3) higher knowledge, including self-realization (*jñāna-mārga*). The *first* path is without any desire for fruits of action, but one must act righteously; the *second* moves toward an everlasting communion with the divine; the *third*, leads to an obliteration of ignorance or imperfect knowledge of the self and all that is nonself, and eventually to a spiritual experience of the nonduality of the self and the Absolute. Traditional "sciences"—be they astronomy, mathematics, medicine, plant science, or ecological concerns—were fostered as means to attaining higher knowledge. They did not develop to have an independent existence of their own; nor were they antagonistic to religion or religious attitude.

In fact, their origins owed not a little to the Hindu religious practices. In the Vedic period, astronomy was mainly pursued for the determination of accurate time, both solar and lunar, for the performance of sacrifices and other rituals, festivals, sowing of seeds, harvesting, and the like. Sacrificial rites, if conducted during auspicious times, were considered to be the media for forging a relationship of microcosm with macrocosm. Early mathematical, especially geometrical, knowledge was gained by the construction of sacrificial altars of prescribed dimensions, and such dimensions had religious significance. Later mathematics evolved as an adjunct to astronomy to meet the latter's requirements for the accurate determination of time and movements of planets. The planets, too, acquired religious significance.

The medical system, *Ayurveda*, had as one of its foundational ideas the *loka-puruṣa-sāmya*, or the harmonious balance between man and nature. Certain medicinal herbs were regarded as being divine healers. Medicinal chemistry (*rasaśāstra*) involving the preparation of minerals and metals by elaborate processings developed in a Tāntrik, or religiously esoteric, ambience. Traditional techniques like icon-casting, cosmetics and perfumery, and dyes and pigments served as accessories for augmenting the religious mood, in the context of practices of worship in temples and, through them, sought to engender the human-divine relationship. Such relationship was also the goal of devotional movements that gathered momentum from about the seventh century A.D. onward, drawing into their fold the vast mass of people. They heightened the cravings of people toward communion with God.

One of the seminal ideas of Hindu thought-structure is the fourfold goal of human life: *dharma* (righteous thinking and action), *artha* (acquiring necessary means for a value-based living), *kāma* (desires, but with detachment), and *mokśa* (emancipation from bondage through spiritualization). Significantly, traditional scientific texts refer to these goals in one form or the other and reveal the religious nature amid their scientific attainments.

Over the ages, Hindu culture has been one of selective assimilation of ideas and practices of other cultures, discarding the barriers of religion and region. The earliest religious composition, Ṛgveda (ca. 1500 B.C.), set the tone by exhorting, "Let noble thoughts come from anywhere, unhindered and overflowing" (I.89.1). The scientific tradition was no exception. Hindu astronomy absorbed certain parameters of Hellenistic astronomy as early as one or two centuries before the Christian era. The seed ideas of Hindu medicinal chemistry owed not a little to the Chinese alchemical concepts and practices around the fourth century A.D. In the medieval period, the Greco-Arabic medicinal system, called *Unāni* in India, was fostered side by side with Ayurveda, and there were mutual assimilations. More important, when Western science with its own methodology was introduced into India mainly by the British in the nineteenth century, Hindus began to assimilate it.

Advent of Modern Science

It is desirable, indeed necessary, to understand the social climate vis-à-vis the advent and growth of (Western) modern science in India. For, like the other non-Christian cultures, India too was not the originator of modern science; nor did it participate in, or contribute to, the early development of modern science that came up in Europe from the fourteenth to fifteenth centuries onward. By that time, over the preceding several centuries, India had developed its geocentric astronomy, blazed new trails in mathematics, and codified its medicinal concepts. Of them, it was only the decimal place value system using nine digits and zero, as developed in India, that was transmitted to Europe through the Islamic savants like al-Khwārizmī and al-Bīrūnī. This introduced a new algorithm during the European Renaissance. The perplexing questions were: Why did the Indian scholars in astronomy, mathematics, and medicine choose to move along the already-charted grooves? Why did they not experiment with new ideas? What was it that circumscribed them to prefer tradition to innovation? Such questions also have relevance to Islamic and Chinese culture.

As for Indian culture, precise answers to these questions are difficult. However, one may find some shades of answers, if one reflects over such factors as the absence of a dominant philosophy of nature, compulsions of orthodox education through the tradition-bound preceptor-disciple relationship, nonemergence of medieval universities of the type that dotted Europe between the thirteenth and fifteenth centuries, social rigidity of caste-governed professionalism, frequent political upheavals with attendant situations of instability, lack of adventurous spirit to go to far-off lands motivated by a desire to expand the horizon of knowledge, nonexistence of an independent, resourceful middle class to support innovative thinkers, and the like.

A question that is germane to this presentation is: did the religious tradition and the attitude of so-called otherworldliness come by way of new thinking and innovations? True, there were different views and approaches to the conception of God as creator and benefactor. There were, then as now, a plethora of anthropomorphic gods, whose worship and superstitious practices might well have acted as a serious drag on the effervescence of innovative spirit. The attitude of "otherworldiness" would also have contributed its share. These may appear to be plausible, but if one examines in-depth the multi-level growth of modern science in India over the last one hundred years or so, in a more or less identical religious environment, it will be rather difficult to accept the view that religion and religious practices were such that they really impeded the growth of innovative scientific pursuits.

In any case, India was the recipient of what was in the nineteenth century generally referred to as Western science. The center of scientific activity lay in the far-off West, and India was on the distant periphery. As it happened, Western science was introduced into India largely by the British, but this introduction was in pursuance of their enlightened self-interest, both as traders and as colonial rulers. One notices three phases of modern science in India. In the first phase, the European naturalists, who were a part of the colonial establishment, were engaged by themselves in the scientific surveys of the new land for exploiting its natural wealth—its minerals, flora, and fauna, and its expertise in arts and crafts. In the second phase, several Indians also became involved with them. For this purpose, they needed scientific and technical education—schools, colleges and universities that came up in different parts of India. In the third phase, (from the last quarter of the nineteenth century until independence), there emerged some Indian pioneers and other leaders who, with their acumen and national spirit, engendered the upwelling of creative science and an innovative climate. Some of them scaled peaks of excellence in the then-frontier areas of science, and one of them earned a Nobel Prize in physics (1930), even in the colonial milieu.

The British rulers did not, as a policy, interfere with the religious ideas and practices of Indians, in their endeavors either to promote scientific education or scientific research organizations. Indian scientific pioneers, too, did not embark upon their pursuits with an outright condemnation of the religious undercurrents of diverse nature. The result was that scientific pursuits and religious practices coexisted without any conflict. The religious tradition continued to be on its own track. The new entrant, science, with its powerful methodology (deduction, mathematical modeling, verifiability, reproducibility, and even falsifiability) and versatile instrumentation did in no way influence or interdict the religious fervor of people. Nor did the religious leaders in particular regard the new entrant as something alien to their own ethos, to their own faiths and beliefs in divine dispensation. Instead, they welcomed the emergence of scientific education and other scientific pursuits with open-mindedness.

Complementarity of Science and Spirituality/Religion

With the attainment of India's independence in the mid-1947, science and its applications began to assume new dimensions. Science and technology were to play, then as now, an effective role in the socioeconomic transformation of the vast poverty-stricken masses, in the enrichment of material life in a planned manner. The successive five-year plans incorporated science and technology in their economic strategies. The importance of the latter was recognized in such a way that the political leadership committed the nation, as it were, to the development of science by the adoption of a Scientific Policy Resolution (1958) in the Parliament. A technology policy, too, was pursued with renewed vigor. Promotion of a scientific attitude became one of the duties under the political constitution of India. As a result, over the last six decades, India's spectrum of science has been an impressive one: a large number of educational and research institutions, scientific agriculture, atomic energy, space technology, medical research, biotechnology, electronics, information technology, industrial research and development, and others. India's science and technology manpower is the third largest in the world.

It is strange but true that, even amid the expanding scientific and technological environs, diverse religious practices are on a scale that is in no way less than what was prevalent before the advent and growth of modern science in India. Even now, people's faith in God, in a supernatural force, seems to be on the increase in tandem, as it were, with their equally increasing confidence in science and technology for improving the material quality of life. There does not appear to be any type of confrontation between science and religion in India. The two are regarded as being complementary to each other, in the context of the values of life that Hinduism, like any other religion, advocates, and the quality of material life that the applications of science try to enrich.

There is another aspect of science and religion in the Indian context, as elsewhere. That is the synergy of science and spirituality. Spirituality is the purest distillate of religious fervor. Religion is to be viewed in its twin facets: one of fostering values of life like love, compassion, truthfulness, nonviolence, nonpossession, and human fellowship, and the other, the pursuit of spirituality toward an experience of undifferentiated concordance with the macrocosm. All religions, irrespective of their labels, have been preaching and promoting these values as cementing bonds among all human beings. Bereft of them, human life is arid; with them, the dividing labels of religions look apparent and not real. Man overcomes such boundaries, becomes human. Religious fervor stimulates spirituality. Spirituality, in turn, radiates humanism.

It is now being increasingly recognized even by distinguished scientists that science, though enormously productive and useful, is not the sole foundation of human life as a whole. With its own limitations, methodological as well as operational, science needs a spirituality that permeates human thoughts and practices, that meets the innermost needs of human spirit. Each is incomplete without the other; each supplements the other towards a value-based life.

The human mind has two dimensions: one, toward sensorial but insatiable desires; the other, transcending the senses and, traversing the religious pathway, for attaining spiritual vision. It is only the religious/spiritual pursuit that leads to a meaningful life, to a human-divine communion. It needs to be recognized that, as Julian Huxley has pointed out, religion is a natural product of human nature and "one could say that religion is innate to human existence itself"[1] Science, too, is a product of human mind, but the way in which it has progressed over the past century and a half shows that it has confined itself to the sensorial realm. The real potential of science lies in its methodology, fortified with sophisticated instruments which are in essence a precise extension of the sensorial interaction with the knowable world. Scientific method is perhaps the best for a consensual or acceptable understanding of nature in all of its manifestations. But to live together in harmony, and to lead a value-based life, one not only notices the inadequacy of science but also feels the necessity of fostering religious spiritual attitude. Few will deny that the scientific and religious spiritual attitudes reflect, respectively, the sensorial and transcendental dimensions of the human mind.

Yoga

Spiritual pursuit is by no means an easy one. It is a continuous tuning of the mind to an exalted and ennobling experience. In this respect, there is an important form of Indian traditional practice called *Yoga,* a spiritual discipline. This can be practiced by anyone, regardless of religion, color, or sex.

Yoga has found adherents not only in all segments of Indian society but has also become widely popular outside India. Yoga, literally means "to yoke," "to unite," or "the union itself." It comprises systematic or well-orchestrated psychophysiological exercises as well as a conscious control of instinctual yearnings. Ultimately, it aims at the elevation of the human mind, and surrendering to a higher being toward the attainment of Oneness and away from the agonizing state of unreal plurality. It leads to a reordering of one's equation with the external world. The doctrine and practice of Yoga comprise eight "limbs":

1. Self-restraint or abstinence (*yama*);
2. Observances in practice (*niyama*);

3. Physical or bodily postures (*āsana*);
4. Technique of rhythmic breathing or breath control (*prāṇāyāma*); temporary cessation of breath in inhalation, exhalation or between inhalation and exhalation;
5. Withdrawal of senses (*pratyāhāra*);
6. Concentration of mind on a limited object, image, or word (*dhāraṇa*);
7. Prolongation of this technique and contemplation without interruption (*dhyāna*);
8. Pure, undifferentiated awareness (*samādhi*) and the disappearance of the notion of "I" or the ego—trance.

Of the foregoing eight limbs as enunciated in the *Yogasūtras* of Patañjali, the first two are essentially ethical in content, namely, abstention from violence and falsehood, nonacquisition, contentment, austerity, and self-surrender to a higher Will. The third relates to the right tuning of the body. The fourth is rhythmic breathing or breath control, an important aspect of Yoga that catalyzes the union of body and mind. The fifth is the full control of the play of senses. All of which are psychophysical. The sixth, seventh, and the eighth are the three meditative states to be attained progressively with deep concentration. Through these, a dedicated practitioner would be able to discard or extinguish the activities of the mind such as emotional stress, anxieties, direct sensorial activities and perturbations, illusory content of our consciousness, horrid memory traces, and the like.

Yoga thus is a pathway to mind-body concord and even beyond, into liberation from the material bondages. It is a spiritual discipline that needs to be adopted with determination. Yoga perhaps may not pass the rigorous scientific tests of verifiability and reproducibility. However, it is important to note that a large number of Yogic practitioners all over the world testify to its efficacy and the positive effect of controlled breathing on mental concentration as well as the benefit of meditation for the equanimity of the human mind. Yogic pursuits can serve as a method for personality reconstruction with controlled desires. According to a recent review that appeared in the *Wall Street Journal,* roughly 15 million U.S. adults now practice Yoga and aver that Yoga sets right various types of disorders, helps relieve tension, and frees one from the cobweb of material life that ensnares man and distracts him from spiritual quest.[2] The tradition of Yoga has a wide base in India among scientists, technologists, public leaders, and common people as an overarching bridge between science and spirituality.

There is no denying that the future of our civilization depends upon the way in which science and religion become the warp and weft of the fabric of civilization. In India, there is now an increasing awareness among scientists, technologists, and other intellectuals, as well as public and religious leaders, of the imperative need for promoting the synergy of science and spirituality for a meaningful, harmonious life. Hinduism is a way of holistic living with immense faith in God. Science and its applications have become integral components of this type of living, without in any way eroding people's faith in God.

Notes

1. Julian Huxley, *Science, Religion, and Human Nature* (London: Watts & Co., 1930), 21.
2. Cited in *Times of India*, Bangalore Edition, October 16, 2003.

10

Science and Buddhism

AT THE CROSSROADS

TRINH XUAN THUAN

Are There Grounds for a Dialogue?

Science and Buddhism have radically different methods for investigating reality. In science, intellect and reason have the leading roles. Science gathers knowledge about the world and condenses that knowledge into laws that can be tested. By dividing, categorizing, analyzing, comparing, and measuring, scientists express these laws in the highly abstract language of mathematics. Intuition is not absent in science, but it gives results only if it can be formulated in a coherent mathematical structure and validated by observation and analysis. By contrast, intuition—or inner experience—plays the leading role in the way Buddhism approaches reality. Buddhism adopts a contemplative approach with an essentially inward gaze while science looks outward. Buddhism is mainly concerned with our inner self while science's main preoccupation is the external world. Rather than breaking up reality in its different components like science does in its reductionist method, Buddhism with its holistic approach aims to understand it in its entirety. Buddhism has no use for measuring apparatus, and does not rely on the sort of sophisticated observations that form the basis of experimental science. Its statements are more qualitative than quantitative.

But the main difference between the pursuit of knowledge in science versus the same pursuit in Buddhism is their ultimate goals. The purpose of science is to find out about the world of phenomena. Its main focus is the understanding of the physical universe, considered to be quantifiable and objective, so as to gain control over the natural world. In Buddhism, on the other hand, knowledge is acquired essentially for therapeutic purposes. The objective is not to find out about the physical world for its own sake, but to free ourselves from the suffering that is caused by our undue attachment to the apparent reality of the external world. Empirical inquiry motivated only by intellectual curiosity is not a principal Buddhist aim. Rather, it wants to understand the true nature of the world to clear away the mists of ignorance and open the way to Enlightenment and the path to liberation. Instead of telescopes, particle accelerators, or microscopes, Buddhism uses the mind as the instrument to investigate the universe. It stresses the importance of elucidating the nature of the mind through direct contemplative experience. Over the centuries it has devised a profound and rigorous approach to the understanding of mental states and of the ultimate nature of the mind. The mind is behind every experience in life. It determines the way we see the world. It takes only the slightest change in our minds, in how we deal with mental states and perceive people and things, for "our" world to be turned completely upside-down. Thus, instead of focusing exclusively on the objective third-person aspect of the world, as classical science does, Buddhism puts also the emphasis on its first-person aspect.

Given these seemingly profound differences in their methods and aims, can there a basis for a dialogue between science and Buddhism? Would Buddhism have something to say about the nature of phenomena as this is not its main interest, whereas such preoccupations lie at the heart of science? The answer to these questions is an unequivocal yes. One of Buddhist philosophy's main tasks is the study of the nature of reality. While science isn't Buddhism's main preoccupation, it has long been asking questions that are astonishingly similar to those that preoccupy modern science. Can separate, indivisible particles be the fundamental building blocks of the world? Do they really exist, or are they just concepts that help us understand reality? Are the laws of physics immutable, and do they have an intrinsic existence, like Platonic ideals? Is there a solid reality behind appearances? What is the origin of the world of phenomena, the world that we see as "real" around us? What is the relationship between the animate and the inanimate, between the subject and the object? What is the nature of space and time? Buddhist philosophers have been studying and pondering these questions for the last twenty-five hundred years. Buddhist literature abounds with logical treatises discussing theories of perception and analyses of different levels of the world of phenomena. It includes many psychological treatises that explore various aspects of consciousness and the ultimate nature of our minds.

And while the investigative methods of Buddhism and science for exploring the world may look, at first glance, very different, a closer look reveals that Buddhism, just like science, relies also on the experimental method to find out about reality. The Buddhist method of analysis often makes use of "thought experiments" that are also widely used in science. These are hypothetical experiments conducted in the mind, which lead to irrefutable conclusions, although the experiments are not actually carried out. This technique has often been used by the best practitioners of science, in particular by Albert Einstein. For example, when studying the nature of space and time, the physicist imagined himself astride a particle of light. When thinking about gravity, he saw himself in an accelerating elevator. In the same manner, Buddhist scholars use thought experiments to dissect reality. Buddhism also resembles science in that it encourages skepticism in the prevailing beliefs. Buddha encourages us not to accept his teachings on faith, but only after thinking them through ourselves. He tells us, "Just as the wise accept gold after testing it by heating, cutting, and rubbing it, so are my words to be accepted after examining them, but not out of respect for me."[1] If we take "science" to mean "a system of knowledge that is rigorous, coherent, and verifiable" or "a set of principles and procedures which involves the recognition and formulation of a problem, the formulation of hypotheses and the collection of data through observation and experiment to test these hypotheses,"[2] then Buddhism can be described as a "contemplative science" or a "science of the mind." But here the field of investigation is not only the "objective" material world that can be physically studied, measured, and calculated, a world that can be described only in terms of third-person quantitative methods. It is enlarged to the whole scope of our "subjective" living experience including mental phenomena, which can only be perceived through first-person introspective observation.

In the remainder of this chapter, I compare the views of reality as seen through the lenses of science and Buddhism. I attempt to build gentle bridges between the sciences of the physical world and the science of the mind. My purpose here is not to make science sound mystical nor to justify Buddhism's underpinnings with the discoveries of modern science.

Science functions well and is perfectly self-sufficient and accomplishes well its stated aim without the need of a philosophical support from Buddhism or from any other religion. In fact, it is when religion thinks it can tell the "truth" to science that problems arise, as in the disastrous condemnation of Galileo by the church in 1633. Buddhism is a science of the Awakening, and whether it is the Earth that goes around the Sun or the contrary cannot have any consequence on its philosophical basis. It has been in existence for some twenty-five hundred years while modern science did not get its start until the sixteenth century. But because both are quests for the truth, and both use criteria of authenticity, rigor, and logic to attain it, their respective worldviews should not result in an insuperable opposition, but rather in a harmonious complementarity. The physicist Werner Heisenberg expressed this view eloquently: "I consider the ambition of overcoming opposites, including also a synthesis embracing both rational understanding and the mystical experience of unity, to be the 'mythos', spoken or unspoken, of our present day and age."[3]

I discuss and compare the worldviews of science and Buddhism by examining in turn each of the three basic tenets of Buddhism. I consider first the concept of impermanence and then address interdependence and vacuity. Then I consider how, in contrast to theist religions, Buddhism rejects the concept of a God or a Creator, and finally I offer concluding remarks in the final section.

Impermanence at the Heart of Reality

Buddhism distinguishes two types of impermanence. First is the gross impermanence, which includes all the obvious changes of persons and things that we witness in our daily lives: the changing of seasons, the erosion of mountains, the passage from youth to old age, our varying emotions. Then there is the subtle impermanence: at each infinitesimal moment, everything that seems to exist changes. The universe is not made of solid, distinct entities but is like a vast stream of events and dynamic currents that are all interconnected and constantly interacting. This concept of perpetual and omnipresent change in Buddhism is in accord with the underlying theme of evolution in all of twentieth-century science.

Consider modern cosmology: Aristotle's immutable heavens and Newton's static universe are no more. Everything is changing and moving, everything is impermanent, from the tiniest elementary particle to the entire universe, including galaxies, stars, planets, and mankind. The universe is not static, but expanding because of the initial impulse it received from its primordial explosion. This dynamic nature is described by the equations of general relativity. With the big bang theory, the universe is not any more eternal. It has a beginning, a past, a present, and a future. It has acquired a history. According to the latest observations, it will expand forever, cooling ever more and die in an icy freeze. In addition to the motion of expansion, all of the universe's structures—asteroids, comets, planets, stars, galaxies, and galaxy clusters—are in perpetual motion and take part in an immense cosmic ballet. They rotate about their axes, revolve around each other, fall toward or move away from one another. They, too, have a history. They are born, reach maturity, then die. Stars have life cycles that span millions, or even billion of years.

Change and evolution have also entered other fields of science. In geology, the continents that were thought to be attached solidly to the Earth's crust are now known to move several centimeters per year, creating volcanoes and earthquakes at the boundaries where the continental plates meet. The surface of the Earth is constantly changing and remodeling itself. As for the biological sciences, the concept of evolution was ushered in by the naturalist Charles Darwin in 1859. Humans have no longer a divine lineage. They are not the descendants of Adam and Eve, themselves created by God, as thought before, but the product of a long evolution shaped by natural selection. Going back in time, man's ancestors are, in turn, primates, reptiles, fishes, invertebrates, and primitive unicellular organisms.

Impermanence rules not only the macroscopic world, but also the atomic and subatomic domains. Particles can modify their nature: a quark can change its family or "flavor"; a proton can become a neutron while emitting a positron and a neutrino. Matter and antimatter can annihilate each other to become pure energy. The energy of motion of a particle can be transformed into another particle, or vice versa; that is, an object's property can become an object. The electrons in the objects that surround us are never still. At this very moment, there are billions of fleeting neutrinos that go through my body every second. Because of the quantum uncertainty of energy, the space around us is filled with an unimaginable number of "virtual" particles, with fleeting ghostlike existences. Constantly appearing and disappearing, they are a perfect illustration of impermanence with their infinitely short life cycles. There is not any doubt: the "subtle impermanence" of Buddhism is everywhere in the description that modern science gives of reality.

The Interdependence and Nonseparability of Phenomena

The Middle Way

The concept of interdependence lies at the heart of the Buddhist vision of the nature of reality. It says that "nothing exists inherently, or can be its own cause." An object can be defined only in terms of other objects and exist only in relationship to others. In other words, *this* arises because *that* exists. Interdependence is essential to the manifestation of phenomena. Our daily experience makes us think that things possess a real, objective independence, as though they exist all on their own and have intrinsic identities. But Buddhism maintains that this way of seeing phenomena is just a mental construct. It calls this perception of distinct phenomena resulting from isolated causes and conditions as "relative truth" or "delusion." Rather it adopts the notion of mutual causality: an event can happen only because it is dependent on other factors. Because everything is part of the whole, nothing can happen separately. Any given thing in our world can appear only because it is connected, conditioned, and in turn conditioning, copresent and cooperating in constant transformation. An entity that exists independently of all others as an immutable and autonomous entity couldn't act on anything, or be acted on itself.

Buddhism thus sees the world as a vast flow of events that are linked together and participate in one another. The way we perceive this flow crystallizes certain aspects of the nonseparable universe, thus creating the illusion that there are autonomous entities that are completely distinct from each other and totally separate from us. Thus phenomena are simply events that happen in some circumstances. This view does not mean that Buddhism denies conventional truth—the sort that ordinary people perceive or the scientist detects with his apparatus—or that it contests the laws of cause and effect, or the laws of physics and mathematics. It simply holds that, if we dig deep enough, there is a difference between the way we see the world and the way it really is.

The most subtle aspect of interdependence concerns the relationship between a phenomenon's designation base and its designation. An object's designation bases refer to its position, dimension, form, color, or any other of its apparent characteristics. Together, they form the object's designation, a mental construct which assigns an autonomous distinct reality to that object. In our everyday experience, when we see an object, we aren't struck by its nominal existence, but by its designation. Because we experience it, Buddhism does not say that the object doesn't exist. But neither does it say that the object possesses an intrinsic reality. It has the view that the object exists (thus avoiding the nihilism that Westerners have sometime mistakenly attributed to Buddhism), but that this existence is purely interdependent. This is what the Buddha calls the Middle Way. A phenomenon with no autonomous existence, but that is nevertheless not totally inexistent, can thus act and function according to the laws of causality.

The Nonlocality of the Quantum World

A notion strikingly similar to that of Buddhism's interdependence is the concept of nonseparability or nonlocality in quantum mechanics. This was revealed by the famous thought experiment designed by Einstein, Podolsky, and Rosen (EPR) in 1935 in an attempt to show that the probabilistic interpretation of quantum mechanics is wrong, and that the theory is incomplete. In simplified terms, the thought experiment goes as follows: Imagine a particle that disintegrates spontaneously into two photons, A and B. The laws of symmetry dictate that they will travel in opposite directions. If A goes westward, then we will detect B to the east. It all seems perfectly normal. But that's forgetting the strangeness of the quantum world. Like Janus, light is double-faced. It can be either wave or particle. Before being captured by the detector, quantum theory tells us that A has the appearance of a wave. This wave being not localized, there was a nonzero probability that A may be found in any direction. It's only when it has been captured that A "learns" that it is moving westward. But, if A didn't "know" before being captured which direction it had taken, how could B have "guessed" what A was doing and adjusted its behavior accordingly so that it could be captured at the same time in the opposite direction? This is impossible, unless A can inform

B instantaneously of the direction it has taken. This would imply a light signal propagating at infinite speed, which would be in contradiction with general relativity. Because "God does not send telepathic signals" and there can be "no spooky action at a distance," Einstein concluded that quantum mechanics did not provide a complete description of reality, that A must "know" which direction it is going to take and "tell" B before they split up. He thought that each particle possesses hidden variables that quantum theory did not take into account, hence its incompleteness.

For nearly thirty years, the EPR experiment remained as a thought experiment because physicists did not know how to carry it out in practice. It was not until 1964 that the physicist John Bell found a way to transform the central idea of EPR from a metaphysical speculation to a proposition that can tested in the laboratory. He devised a mathematical theorem now called "Bell's inequality" that could be verified experimentally if particles really did have hidden variables. At the beginning of the 1980s, the technology was finally ripe for the physicist Alain Aspect and his team in Paris to carry out a series of experiments on pair of entangled photons (that is, photons that have interacted with each other). They found that Bell's inequality was always violated, meaning that there are no hidden variables. Quantum mechanics was right, and Einstein was wrong. In Aspect's experiments, photons A and B were twelve meters apart, yet B always "knew" instantaneously what A was doing, and reacted accordingly. The physicists were sure that no light signal could have been exchanged between A and B because atomic clocks, connected to the detectors that capture A and B, allow them to gauge the moment of each photon's arrival extremely accurately. The difference between the two arrival times is less than a few tenths of a billionth of a second; it is probably zero, in fact, but existing atomic clocks don't allow us to measure periods of under 10^{-10} seconds. Now, in 10^{-10} seconds, light can travel only three centimeters, far less than the twelve meters separating A from B. What is more, the result is the same if the distance between the two entangled photons is increased. In the latest experiment carried out in 1998 by the physicist Nicolas Gisin and his colleagues in Geneva, the photons are separated by ten kilometers, yet their behaviors are perfectly correlated. This is paradoxical only if, like Einstein, we think that reality is cut up and localized in each photon. The problem goes away if we admit that A and B, once they have interacted with each other, become part of a nonseparable reality, no matter how far apart they are, even if they are at opposite ends of the universe. A does not need to send a signal to B because they share the same reality. Quantum mechanics thus eliminates all idea of locality and provides a holistic view of space. For two entangled photons, the notions of "here" and "there" become meaningless because here is identical to there. That is what physicists call the nonseparability or nonlocality of space, which is akin to the concept of the interdependence of phenomena in Buddhism.

Foucault's Pendulum and the Interdependence of the Macrocosm

Another famous and fascinating physics experiment shows that the interdependence of phenomena isn't limited to the world of particles but pervades the whole universe. This is the pendulum experiment carried out by the physicist Léon Foucault in 1851 at the Panthéon in Paris to demonstrate the rotation of the Earth. We are all familiar with the behavior of the pendulum. As time passes, the direction in which it swings changes. If it was set swinging in a north-south direction, after a few hours, it is swinging east-west. If the pendulum were placed at either the North or the South Pole, it would turn completely around in twenty-four hours (in Paris, because of a latitude effect, Foucault's pendulum performs only part of a complete rotation in a day). Foucault realized that, in fact, the pendulum swung in the same direction, and it was the Earth that turned.

But there remains a puzzle not clearly understood to this day. The swing of the pendulum is fixed in space, but fixed with respect to what? The pendulum is attached to a building that is itself attached to Earth. The Earth carries us at some 30 kilometers per second (km/s) around the Sun, which is itself flying through space at 230 km/s in its orbit around the center of the Milky Way. Our galaxy is in turn falling toward the Andromeda galaxy at some 90 km/s. The Local Group of galaxies, the most massive members of which are the Galaxy and Andromeda, is moving at 600 km/s under the gravitational attraction of the Virgo cluster and of the Hydra-Centaurus supercluster. The latter is itself falling toward the Great Attractor, the mass of which is equivalent to that of tens of thousands of galaxies. Is the behavior of Foucault's pendulum dictated by any of these relatively nearby structures? In order to find out which celestial object controls the swing of the pendulum, we simply set the pendulum swinging in that celestial object's direction. If, as that object moves in the sky, it always remains in the plane of the pendulum's swing, then we can say that the object is responsible for the pendulum's behavior. Let's swing the pendulum in the direction of the Sun. After a month, our star has already shifted by a whole 15° away from the pendulum's direction of swing. Let's now point the pendulum toward the nearest star, Proxima Centauri, which is four light-years away. The star stays longer in the swing plane, but after several years, ends up drifting away. The Andromeda galaxy, which is 2.3 million light-years away, moves away more slowly, but does drift off the plane. The time spent in line with the pendulum's swing grows longer and the shift becomes smaller, the greater the distance of the celestial object. Only the most distant galaxies, situated at the edge of the known universe, billions of light-years away, do not drift away from the plane of the pendulum's swing.

The conclusion we must draw is extraordinary: Foucault's pendulum doesn't base its behavior on its local environment, but rather on the most distant galaxies, or, more accurately, on the entire universe, given that practically all visible matter is to be found in distant galaxies and not in nearby stars. Thus, what happens here on Earth is decided by all the vast cosmos. What occurs on our tiny planet depends on all the structures in the universe.

Why does the pendulum behave in such a way? We don't know. The physicist Ernst Mach thought it could be explained by a sort of omnipresence of matter and its influence. According to Mach, an object's mass—that is to say, the amount of its inertia, or resistance to movement—comes from the influence of the entire universe through a mysterious interaction, different from gravity, which he did not specify. No one else has managed to do so since. Just as the EPR experiment forces us to accept that interactions exist in the microcosm that are different from those described by known physics, Foucault's pendulum does the same for the macrocosm. Such interactions are not based on a force or an exchange of energy, and they connect the entire universe. Again, we are drawn to a conclusion that resembles very much Buddhism's concept of interdependence: each part contains the whole, and each part depends on all the other parts.

Emptiness or the Absence of an Intrinsic Reality

The notion of interdependence leads us directly to the third key idea of Buddhism (the two others being impermanence and interdependence):

that of emptiness or vacuity. Since everything is interdependent, nothing can be self-defining and exist inherently. The idea of intrinsic properties that exist in themselves and by themselves must be thrown out. When Buddhism states that emptiness is the ultimate nature of things, it means that the things we see around us, the phenomena of our world, lack any autonomous or permanent existence. Here "emptiness" does not mean nothingness, void, or absence of phenomena, as early Western commentators on Buddhism thought, but the absence of inherent existence. Buddhism does not espouse any form of nihilism. Emptiness does not correspond to nonexistence. If you can't speak of real existence, you can't speak of nonexistence either. Thus, according to Buddhism, learning to understand the essential unreality of things is an integral part of the spiritual way. Emptiness isn't just the true nature of phenomena, it's also the potential that allows the manifestation of an infinite variety of phenomena. To quote the second-century Buddhist master Nagarjuna: "Since all is empty, all is possible," or the famous scripture Perfection of Wisdom: "Though phenomena appear, they are empty; though empty, they appear." If reality were permanent, and its properties too, then nothing would change. Phenomena could not appear. But because things have no intrinsic reality, they can have infinite manifestations.

On the subject of the absence of an intrinsic reality, quantum physics has once again something strikingly similar to say. According to Niels Bohr and Werner Heisenberg, the main proponents of what is called "the Copenhagen interpretation" of quantum mechanics, we can no longer talk about atoms and electrons as being real entities with well-defined properties, such as speed and position, tracing out equally well-defined trajectories. We must consider them as part of a world made up of potentialities and not of objects and facts. Light and matter can be said to have no intrinsic reality because they have a dual nature: they can appear either as waves or particles depending on the measuring apparatus. The phenomenon that we call a photon is a wave when the measuring machine is shut off and we are not observing it. But as soon as the apparatus is activated and a measurement is made, it takes the appearance of a particle. The particle and wave aspects cannot be dissociated. On the contrary, they complement each other. This is what Bohr calls the "principle of complementarity." Thus, the very nature of light and matter is subject to interdependent relationships. It is no longer intrinsic but changes depending on the interaction between the observer and the object under observation. To speak of a particle's intrinsic reality, or the reality it possesses when unobserved, is meaningless because we can never apprehend it. Thus for Bohr, the "atom" concept is merely a convenient picture that helps physicists put together diverse observations of the particle world into a coherent and logical scheme. He emphasized the impossibility of going beyond the results of experiments and measurements: "In our description of nature, the purpose is not to disclose the real essence of phenomena, but only to track down, so far as possible, relations between the manifold aspects of our experience."[4] Erwin Schrödinger also warned us against a materialistic view of atoms and their constituents: "It is better not to view a particle as a permanent entity, but rather as an instantaneous event. Sometimes these events link together to create the illusion of permanent entities."[5] Quantum mechanics has radically revised our conception of an object, by making it subordinate to a measurement or, in other words, an event. Just as in Buddhism, only relationships between objects exist, but not the objects themselves.

In Search of the Great Watchmaker

The Fine-Tuning of the Universe

Modern cosmology has discovered that the conditions that allow for life and intelligence to emerge in the universe seem to be coded in the properties of each atom, star, and galaxy in the cosmos and in all of the physical laws that govern it. The universe appears to have been very finely tuned in order to produce an intelligent observer capable of appreciating its organization and harmony. This statement is the basis of the anthropic principle from the Greek *anthropos*, which means "person." Concerning the anthropic principle, there are two remarks to be made. First, the definition I gave above concerns only the "strong" version of the anthropic principle. There is also a "weak" version that doesn't presuppose any intention in the design of nature. It almost comes down to a tautology—the properties of the universe must be compatible with the existence of mankind—and I will not discuss it further. Second, the term "anthropic" is really inappropriate as it implies that humanity was the goal toward which the universe has evolved. In fact, anthropic arguments would apply to any form of intelligence in the universe.

What is the scientific basis of the anthropic principle? The way our universe evolved depends on two types of information: (1) its initial conditions, such as its total mass and energy contents, its initial expansion rate, and so forth; and (2) about fifteen physical constants: the gravitational constant, the Planck constant, the speed of light, the masses of the elementary particles, and so forth. We can measure the values of these constants with extreme precision, but we do not have any theory to predict them. By constructing model universes with varying initial conditions and physical constants, astrophysicists have discovered that these need to be fine-tuned to the extreme: if the physical constants and the initial conditions were just slightly different, we wouldn't be here to talk about them. For instance, let's consider the initial density of matter of the universe. Matter has a gravitational pull that counteracts the force of expansion from the big bang and slows down the universe's rate of expansion. If its initial density had been too high, then the universe would have collapsed into itself after a relatively short time—a million years, a century or even just a year, depending on the exact density. Such a time span would have been too short for stars to accomplish their nuclear alchemy and produce heavy elements like carbon, which are essential to life. On the other hand, if the initial density of matter had been too low, then there would not have been enough gravity for stars to form. And no stars, no heavy elements, and no life! Everything hangs on an extremely delicate balance. The initial density of the universe had to be fixed to an accuracy of 10^{-60}. This astonishing precision is analogous to the dexterity of an archer hitting a one-centimeter-square target placed fourteen billion light-years away, at the edge of the observable universe! The precision of the fine-tuning varies, depending on the particular constant or initial condition, but in each case, just a tiny change makes the universe barren, devoid of life and consciousness.

Is There a Principle of Organization?

What are we to make of such an extraordinary fine-tuning? It seems to me that we are faced with two distinct choices: the tuning was the consequence of either chance or necessity, to quote the title of the French biologist Jacques Monod's book.[6] If we opt for chance, then we must postulate the existence of an infinite number of other universes besides our own forming what is called a "multiverse." Each of these universes will have its own combination of physical constants and initial conditions, but ours was the only universe born with just the right combination to have evolved to create life. All the others were losers, and only ours is the winner. If you play the lottery an infinite number of times, then you inevitably end up winning the jackpot. On the other hand, if we reject the hypothesis of a multiverse and postulate that there exists a single universe, ours, then we must postulate the existence of a principle of creation which finely adjusted the evolution of the universe.

How to choose between these two options? Science does not help us here because it allows both possibilities. Concerning the chance option, there are several ways that have been suggested to create a multiverse. For example, to get around the probabilistic description of the quantum world, the physicist Hugh Everett has proposed that the universe splits into as many nearly identical copies of itself as there are possibilities and choices to be made. Some universes would differ only by the position of one electron in one atom, but others would be more radically different. Their physical laws and constants, their initial conditions wouldn't be the same. Another scenario is that of a cyclical universe with an infinite series of big bangs and big crunches. Whenever the universe is reborn from its ashes to begin again in a new big bang, it would start with a new combination of physical constants and initial conditions. Yet another possibility to create a multiverse is the theory proposed by the physicist Andrei Linde and others whereby each of the infinite number of fluctuations of the primordial quantum froth created a universe. Our universe would then be just a tiny bubble in a super-universe made up of an infinite number of other bubbles. Except for our own, none of those universes would harbor intelligent life because their physical constants and laws wouldn't be suitable.

There Is Not a Creator in Buddhism

What is the position of Buddhism regarding the remarkable fine-tuning of the universe? Does it accept the notion of an all-knowing Creator or some sort of principle of creation that finely adjusted the evolution of the universe? Or does it attribute the remarkable harmony and precision of the universe to chance? The question of whether or not there is a creating God is a key point of distinction between Buddhism and the other great spiritual traditions of the world. For Buddhism, the notion of a first cause does not stand up to analysis, and that's because of the concepts of vacuity and interdependence discussed before. Buddhism considers the question of creation irrelevant because according to it, phenomena aren't really born, in the sense that they pass from nonexistence into existence. They exist only in terms of what is called "relative truth" and have no actual reality. Relative, or conventional, truth comes from our experience of the world where we suppose that things exist objectively. Buddhism says that such perceptions are deceptive as, ultimately, phenomena are not objective, that is, they have no intrinsic existence. This is the "absolute truth." In these terms, the question of creation becomes a false problem. The problem of an origin comes about only from a belief in the absolute reality of phenomena. The idea of creation is necessary only if we believe in an objective world. It disappears when we realize that phenomena, although they can be clearly seen, have no separate existence and are not "objective." And if creation is not needed, the idea of a Creator is also not required.

The Buddhist view does not, however, exclude the possibility of the unfolding of the world. Obviously the phenomena we see around us aren't nonexistent, but Buddhism maintains that if we examine how they exist, then we soon see that they can't be viewed as a set of independent entities, each with its own existence. To quote Nagarjuna, the great second-century Indian philosopher: "The nature of phenomena is that of mutual dependence; in themselves, phenomena are nothing at all." Thus, their evolution is neither by chance nor fixed by divine intervention. Instead they follow the laws of cause and effect in a global interdependence and reciprocal causality. Because things have no independent reality, they can't really begin or end as distinct entities. The idea of the universe's beginning and ending belongs to relative, not absolute, truth.

How does this view square with present scientific cosmology? The only sort of universe that would have no beginning nor end would be a cyclical universe, with an infinite series of big bangs and big crunches in the past and in the future. But the scenario of our universe one day collapsing into itself in a big crunch appears to be not in agreement with present-day observations. These say that the mass densities of luminous matter (0.5%

of the total mass and energy content of the universe), dark matter (29.5%) and dark energy (70%) add up to be just the critical density. This means that the geometry of the universe is flat; that is, it will expand forever, its expansion velocity not reaching zero until after an infinite time in the future. Thus, our present state of knowledge seems to exclude the idea of a cyclical universe.

Streams of Consciousness Coexisting with the Material World

How about the anthropic principle? As far as Buddhism is concerned, the extraordinary fine-tuning of the universe for consciousness to emerge is not the work of a Great Watchmaker since the latter does not exist. Nor is it the product of pure chance as suggested by proponents of the multiverse idea: we are here because we just happen to live by chance in the universe with the right combination of physical constants and physical conditions. Buddhism considers that the material universe and consciousness have always coexisted since "beginningless" time. To coexist, phenomena must be mutually suitable, hence the remarkable fine-tuning. The latter arises because matter and consciousness cannot exclude each other, because they are interdependent. How does that point of view chime with modern neurobiology? Biological sciences are still a long way from being able to explain the origin of consciousness. However, the vast majority of biologists think that there is no need to postulate streams of consciousness that coexist with matter. They hold that the former can emerge from the latter, that mind can arise from matter. Consciousness arose once the networks of brain cells in living beings reached a certain threshold of complexity. In their view, consciousness emerged, just as life itself, from the intricate assembly of inanimate atoms.

One question arises: when Buddhism conjectures that consciousness is separate from and transcends the physical, isn't it falling back into Descartes's mind-body dualism, in which there are two distinct types of reality, that of the mind (or thought) and that of the material world? The answer is no. Buddhism's view is radically different from Cartesian dualism. There's merely a conventional difference between matter and consciousness because, in the end, neither of them has an inherent existence. Because Buddhism refutes the ultimate reality of phenomena, it also refutes the idea that consciousness is independent and exists inherently.

Science and Spirituality: Two Windows into Reality

I have attempted above to show striking convergences between the views of reality of Buddhism and modern science. Impermanence, a key Buddhist concept, echoes the concept of evolution in the cosmological, geological, and biological sciences. Nothing is static, everything changes, moves, and evolves, from the tiniest atom to the largest structures in the universe. The universe itself has acquired a history. Darwinian evolution coupled with natural selection rules the constant changes in the living world. The concept of interdependence, which is at the heart of Buddhism, resonates with the globality and nonseparability of space implied by the EPR experiment on the atomic and subatomic scales, and by Foucault's pendulum experiment on the scale of the universe. The Buddhist concept of emptiness, the absence of any permanent and autonomously existing phenomena, finds its scientific equivalent in the dual nature of light and matter in the quantum world. Because a photon is a wave when we do not observe it and a particle when we make a measurement, it can be said not to have an inherent and autonomous existence, its appearance depending on the observer.

I have also pointed out that Buddhism rejects the idea of a beginning of the universe and of a God or a creative principle that fine-tunes its properties to allow the emergence of consciousness. Buddhism considers that consciousness is coexistent with matter but does not derive from it. Because both are mutually interdependent, there is no need to fine-tune the material universe for it to harbor consciousness.

The above convergences are not surprising, given that both science and Buddhism use criteria of rigor and authenticity to attain the truth. Since both aim to describe reality, they must meet on common ground and not be exclusive of each other. Whereas in science the primary methods of discovery are experimentation and theorizing based on analysis, in Buddhism contemplation is the primary method. Both are windows that allow us to peer at reality. They are both valid in their respective domains and complement each other. Science reveals to us "conventional" knowledge. Its aim is to understand the world of phenomena. Its technical applications can have a good or bad effect on our physical existence. Contemplation, however, by helping us to see the true nature of reality, aims to improve our inner selves so that we can act to improve everybody's existence. Scientists use ever more powerful instruments to probe nature. In the contemplative approach, the only instrument is the mind. The contemplative observes how his thoughts are bound together and how they bind him. He examines the mechanisms of happiness and suffering and tries to discover the mental processes that increase his inner peace and make him more open to others in order to develop them, as well as those processes that have a destructive effect in order to eliminate them. Science provides us with information, but brings about no spiritual growth or transformation. By contrast, the spiritual or contemplative approach must lead to a profound personal transformation in the way we perceive the world and act on it. The Buddhist, by realizing that objects have no intrinsic existence, lessens his attachment to them, which diminishes his suffering. The scientist, with the same realization, is content to consider that as an intellectual advance which can be used to further his work, without changing fundamentally his basic vision of the world and how he leads his life.

When faced with ethical or moral issues which, as in the field of genetics, are becoming ever more pressing, science needs the help of spirituality in order not to forget our humanity. Einstein expresses admirably that need for the union of science and spirituality: "The religion of the future will be a cosmic religion. It will have to transcend a personal God and avoid dogma and theology. Encompassing both the natural and the spiritual, it will have to be based on a religious sense arising from the experience of all things, natural and spiritual, considered as a meaningful unity. . . . Buddhism answers this description. . . . If there is any religion that could respond to the needs of modern science, it would be Buddhism."[7]

Notes

1. D. Shastri, *Tattvasamgraha* (Varanasi: Bauddhabharati, 1968), 3587.
2. *Merriam-Webster's Collegiate Dictionary*, 13 ed., "science."
3. Werner Heisenberg, "Wolfgang Pauli's Philosophical Outlook," in *Across the Frontiers* (New York: Harper & Row, 1974), chap. 3.
4. Niels Bohr, *Atomic Theory and the Description of Nature* (Woodbrige, Conn.: Ox Bow Press, 1987), 18.
5. Erwin Schrodinger, *Nature and the Greeks* (Cambridge: Cambridge University Press, 1954), 85.

6. Jacques Monod, *Chance and Necessity* (New York: Alfred A. Knopf, 1971).
7. A. Einstein quoted in Thinley Norbu, "Welcoming Flowers" in *Across the Cleansed Threshold of Hope: An Answer to the Pope's Criticism of Buddhism* (New York: Jewel Publishing House, 1997).

Suggestions for Further Reading

The themes discussed here are developed in greater detail in:

Ricard, M., and T. X. Thuan. *The Quantum and the Lotus*. New York: Crown, 2001. Paperback edition, New York: Three Rivers Press, 2004.

Over the last twenty years, there have been a series of "Mind and Life" meetings between the Dalai Lama and a number of eminent scientists, including neurobiologists, psychiatrists, philosophers, and physicists. The emphasis of these meetings has been mainly on the mind, since Buddhism has devised over twenty-five centuries a profound and rigorous approach to understanding mental states and the ultimate nature of the mind, and can bring much to Western neurobiology. Published accounts of these meetings include:

Goleman, D. *Healing Emotions: Conversations with the Dalai Lama on Mindfulness, Emotions and Health.* Boston: Shambhala Publications, 1997.

———. *Destructive Emotions: A Scientific Dialogue with the Dalai Lama.* New York: Bantam Doubleday, 2002.

Hayward, J. W. *Shifting Worlds, Changing Minds: Where the Sciences and Buddhism Meet.* Boston: Shambhala Publications, 1987.

Houshmand, Z., R. B. Livingston, and B. A. Wallace. *Consciousness at the Crossroads: Conversations with the Dalai Lama on Brainscience and Buddhism.* Ithaca: Snow Lion Publications, 1999.

Varela, F. J. *Sleeping, Dreaming, and Dying: An Exploration of Consciousness with the Dalai Lama.* Boston: Wisdom Publications, 1997.

Varela, F. J., and J. Hayward. *Gentle Bridges: Conversations with the Dalai Lama on the Sciences of Mind.* Boston: Shambhala Publications, 2001.

Zajonc, A. *The New Physics and Cosmology: Dialogues with the Dalai Lama.* New York: Oxford University Press, 2004.

Other works that discuss the relationships between science and Buddhism are:

Wallace, B. A. *The Taboo of Subjectivity: Toward a New Science of Consciousness.* New York: Oxford University Press, 2000.

———. *Buddhism and Science: Breaking New Ground.* New York: Columbia University Press, 2003.

11
Asian Christianity
TOWARD A TRILOGUE OF HUMILITY: SCIENCES, THEOLOGIES, AND ASIAN RELIGIONS

HEUP YOUNG KIM

The Context: Asian Christianity

Asian Christianity is an intricate term. Geographically, Asia refers to a vast land, the largest continent on this planet. Culturally and religiously, Asia is enormously diverse and rich, as Asia is the home of world religions. Not only Siddhartha, Confucius, Lao-Tzu, and Ch'oe che-u, but also Abraham, Moses, Jesus, Paul, and Muhammed were Asians, not Euro-Americans. It is ironic that Christianity is understood as a Western religion and that Christianity in Asia is rather called "Asian" Christianity.

Philip Jenkins said that "the whole idea of 'Western Christianity' distorts the true pattern of the religion's development over time."[1] Western missionary activities, under the assumption of Christianity as "the faith of Europe" and "Europeandom," have, as history attests, been responsible for some grave errors. An African Christian leader stated metaphorically: "When the [European] missionaries came to Africa they had the Bible and we had the land. They said, 'Let us pray.' We closed our eyes. When we opened them we had the Bible and they had the land."[2] In the last century, nonetheless, the religious map of Christianity has dramatically changed. Euro-American Christianity no longer occupies the majority but only a minority of global Christianity. The Christian center of gravity has shifted from Europe toward Africa, Latin America, and Asia. With "the rise of new Christianity," "the myth of Western Christianity" has been completely dispelled.[3]

Nevertheless, the dialogue between religion and science remains very much a Western phenomenon insofar as Western Christian theology is concerned. In this chapter, I explore some different views from the perspective of Asian Christianity. However, this is not a historical survey, nor a study covering all the complexities of Asian Christianity. Rather, I elaborate on some of my reflections based on my limited experiences as a Korean or East Asian Christian.

The Myth of Bridge Building

Western theologians draw upon the metaphor of bridge building to illustrate the relationship between religion and science.[4] However, this metaphor is too romantic and misleading to the eyes of Asian Christians. First of all, theology and science are not two different worlds radically separated by a gulf that must be bridged. It is undeniable that Christianity played at least a crucial role in, if not constituted the religious origin of, the rise of modern science.[5] John Brooke has argued that terms such as "conflict" or "separation," traditionally used in reference to the relationship between science and religion, are historically inadequate.[6] Even Darwinism, Michael Ruse has insisted, can be properly understood in relation to the Judeo-Christian tradition.[7]

In addition, the bridge metaphor betrays a Eurocentric myopia that does not acknowledge the profoundly perplexing diversity of religious understanding.[8] As the perplexities indicate, the *real* gulf exists between science and non-Christian religions. As Wilfred C. Smith predicts, "The impact of agnostic science will turn out to have been as child's play compared to the challenge to Christian theology of the faith of other men."[9]

Furthermore, the bridge-building metaphor is awkward and confusing to the people in Asia. It was, after all, the natural sciences that attracted them when Western missionaries came to the region. Christianity was first welcomed because of the impressive power and advantages of modern science that those missionaries brought with them. For this reason, in this non-Christian world, science has been viewed as an inseparable part of Christianity. Missionaries explicitly used science as a means for their Oriental mission and evangelism. Matteo Ricci (1552–1610), the most notable example, introduced "the emerging physical sciences" as "the foundation for the Christian faith and the revelation of Jesus Christ."[10] The translation of scientific classics such as Euclid's *Elements of Geometry* was part of the program of the Catholic mission in the Chinese world.

Undoubtedly, the role of natural science has not always remained impartial and has been utilized by the Christian West to perpetuate and justify colonialism, orientalism, and cultural imperialism. It is also evident that natural science itself is not neutral but culturally dependent. The metaphor of bridge building is thus not only incorrect but also misleading, because it toadies to the notion of the hegemony of Western scientific thinking. From the vantage point of Asian Christianity, therefore, the Western dialogue between religion and science is subject to a *hermeneutics of suspicion*.

The Third Epoch of Christianity

Ecumenically, Christian theologians throughout Asia assembled for the Congress of Asian Theologians (CATS) in 1997. In its inaugural meeting, signaling the advance of the third epoch of world Christianity, CATS called for "a third generation of missiology that goes beyond the paradigms of mission bequeathed to us by the ecumenical movement and Vatican II."[11] In the third assembly (2002), CATS further announced the following as a concluding statement:

> This Congress aimed at consolidating and advancing the new paradigm of Christian life among the rich variety of religious traditions of Asia. We acknowledge that Christian mission in Asia has been to a great extent a failure if measured by its own aims. The failure emerged from its unhelpful theology of religions and its missiology. . . . However, the experience of God does not need to be imported, for it is already here. God lives and works in the great religions of Asia and also in the folk religions, which often pose a direct challenge to institutional Christianity. Christians now must humbly acknowledge that in these many ways God has always been savingly present in the continent. In its failure to acknowledge these facts, the Christian mission in Asia was arrogant and colonialist. It denied the possibility of pluralism.[12]

Asian theologians called for new paradigms of theology and missiology. In the third epoch of Christianity, apologetic and dogmatic models of theism are inappropriate, anachronistic, and backward. Unfortunately, however, these models seem still to be prevailing in the dialogue between religion and science, as they appear in the theologies of leading figures such as Ian Barbour and John Polkinghorne. In Barbour's pioneering works, apologetics for theism remain at the core of his arguments: "Theism, in short, is not inherently in conflict with science, but it does conflict with a metaphysics of materialism."[13] Polkinghorne's daring reformulation of Orthodox Christian faith (e.g., the Nicene Creed) in the era of science from the perspective of a theoretical physicist has a certain legitimacy within the secularized European context, but is problematic in an Asian context where colonialist missionaries superimposed on Orthodox Christianity with the terrifying threat of gunboats.[14] As CATS stated:

> The modern missionary era in Asia . . . was, to a great extent, a dismal phase with hostile, aggressive, and even arrogant attitudes to the other faiths. The local cultures and religious traditions of Asia were often looked upon as inferior and to be replaced by Christianity and Western cultural traditions. The missionary praxis, in general, was one of converting and baptizing people of other religions and extending the churches at the cost of the social, cultural and religious values that constituted their inherent sense of dignity and identity.[15]

In the eyes of Asian Christians, it looks suspicious that such apologetic and dogmatic paradigms are still prevalent in the dialogue between science and religion. They are, after all, vulnerable for use again as high-tech, missiological, and political plots for evangelism and cultural imperialism in the perpetuation of Western Christian hegemony. Sensitive to the possibility that such missiological fallacies should not be repeated again in the name of "the dialogue between religion and science," Asian Christians thus call for an alternative paradigm of dialogue.

The Interreligious Imperative

The most distinctive religious feature of Asia lies in its plurality of religions where interreligious dialogue and practice are matters of everyday life. For Asian Christians, the notion of "interreligious relations" is not merely some hypothetical construct, but a living reality. As Aloysius Pieris said:

> It is common knowledge that the West studies all the world religions, whereas the East simply practices them. Religion is a department in many a Western university, just as it has been a "department" in life. Among us in the East, however, religion is life. The same is true of inter-religious dialogue: an academic luxury in the West, and a *modus vivendi* in the East. The interfaith encounter with all its psycho-sociological tensions constitutes a day-to-day experience in pluri-religious societies of the Orient.[16]

Furthermore, the phenomenon of religious pluralism is no longer confined to Asia but is, in fact, a global phenomenon. In traditionally Christian cities such as London, Paris, Amsterdam, New York, Los Angeles, Chicago, and San Francisco, it is not at all difficult to find Buddhist Zen centers and people practicing T'ai-chi, Taoism, and Confucianism.[17] Inter-religious dialogue constitutes a significant part of contemporary theology. David Tracy affirmed that "dialogue among religions is no longer a luxury but a theological necessity."[18] More directly, "It is dialogue or die."[19]

The Method: A Trilogue of Humility

A Humble Approach

Interreligious dialogue can offer useful insights into how more appropriate paradigms of dialogue between the religions and the sciences might be developed. As I have suggested elsewhere, a fruitful dialogue can be construed in two methodological stages; namely, "a descriptive-comparative stage" (dialogue) and "a normative-constructive stage" (theology of religion).[20] While comparable to "dialogue" and "integration" (theology of nature) models in the fourfold typology of Barbour, these two stages refer to two different moments of hermeneutics (descriptive vs. normative).

The first, the descriptive-comparative stage requires "an attitude of *reverence*" or epistemological modesty to *respect* views and presuppositions of the other partners.[21] One should be cautious not to superimpose one's categorical schema on others so as not to commit a "fallacy of misplaced concreteness" (Be descriptive, not prescriptive!).[22] To make a dialogue fruitful, one may even need courage to compel an *epoche*, "faithful agnosticism," or a bracketing off of one's own a priori axioms.[23] In this stage, an apologetics for theistic persuasion (Barbour) or a dogmatic proclamation (Polkinghorne) is an inappropriate but risky option. However, theologians must also take care not to fall into the missiological trap of epistemological immodesty or ethical hubris. In deep humility, and even with courage to bracket off their theological agenda if necessary, as in interreligious dialogue, they should open their hearts and listen to the narratives of others.

In the second, normative-constructive stage, however, Christian theologians could have complete freedom to do constructive theology for their faith and their own Christian communities. In this theological stage, a theology of nature or science becomes appropriate and much more sensible. However, it should be pointed out that no theology is absolute and *creatio ex nihilo*. Theologies are inevitably constructed on the basis of theologians' limited religiocultural experiences within their particular social location, and thus carry over inexorably the prejudices and limitations of the theologians who construct them. In this regard, John Templeton appropriately proposed a "humble approach":

> The Theology of Humility encourages thinking which is open minded and conclusions which are qualified with the tentative word "maybe." It encourages change and progress and does not resist any advance in the knowledge of God or of nature, but is always ready to rethink what is known and to revise the assumptions and preconditions behind our knowledge.[24]

In the pluri-religious Asian context, furthermore, the dialogue between religion and science involves dual or multiple interreligious exchanges; that is to say, a trilogue among Christian theologies, Asian religions, and the natural sciences. Within this trilogue, Asian Christianity has the greatest potentiality to enhance and globalize the dialogue between religions and sciences; namely, in and through dialogue with diverse Asian religions such as Hinduism, Buddhism, Confucianism, or Taoism. It is thus proposed that a trilogue of humility, a humble approach of integrated interreligious and interdisciplinary dialogues, constitutes a viable paradigm of future dialogue between the religions and the sciences.

Locus of the Trilogue: The Wisdom (Tao) of Humanization

Often, a comparison between different traditions in terms of concept, methodology, or metaphysics does not progress much beyond a glorified intellectual mind game in which phenomenological parallels of one's dogma and agenda are sought out within the texts of other traditions. Orientalism and postcolonial criticisms have exposed pungent historical errors committed by the Christian West under the guise of crusadic triumphalism.[25] For this reason, any dialogue between the religions and the sciences needs to look for an alternative locus to that of spurious metaphysical conceptuality.

It is more appropriate to regard an encounter between the sciences and religions as a "fusion of hermeneutical horizons."[26] The goal of both the religions and the sciences is, after all, a realization of the full potential of humanity. Therefore, the real meeting point between the sciences and the religions is not so much located within an abstract metaphysics, a methodology of parallelism, or an epistemology of knowledge, but in a hermeneutics of the human person, the way of life, or, more specifically, the ortho-praxis of humanization—that is to say, the tao of how to be fully human.[27] Here we see the significance of East Asian wisdom, the main focus of which is the concrete embodiment of practical wisdom for full humanity in contrast to the speculative postulation of unverifiable supernatural knowledge.

In this regard, Hans Küng made an important correction. Instead of the generally accepted but defective bipolar view of world religions (Middle East and India), he rightly advocated a tripolar view. Judaism, Christianity, and Islam are "the first great river system, of Semitic origin and prophetic character."[28] Hinduism, Buddhism, and other Indian religions are "the second great river system, of Indian origin and mystical character." And, although neglected for a long time, Confucianism and Taoism of East Asian origin are the "third independent religious river system" of sapiential character, "equal in value" but in contrast to the first and the second.

More precisely, Neo-Confucianism, since its appearance in the eleventh century as a Confucian response to Taoism and Buddhism, constitutes the most distinctive and common attribute of the religiocultural matrix of East Asia. It emphasizes the learning of the *tao* (wisdom in the unity of theory and praxis) to attain full humanity in harmony with heaven and the Earth (anthropocosmic vision). The primary objective of Neo-Confucian investigation is seen not so much in the formulation of metaphysics or speculative theory, but in the enlightenment and embodiment of the tao, the ortho-praxis of human life. Neo-Confucianism affirms that one can attain the embodiment of the tao through individually and collectively rigorous practices of self-cultivation in the "concrete-universal" network of relationships.[29]

Sanctification is a doctrine of Christian theology homologically equivalent to this Neo-Confucian notion of self-cultivation. Hence, an ideal locus for Christian interreligious dialogue in East Asia is a faith in radical humanization (orthopraxis)—namely, self-cultivation and sanctification—as opposed to a metaphysics, a psychology, or the philosophy of religion. In a similar manner, an ideal locus for the dialogue between science and religion can be found in the common human quest for the tao—cultivating and sanctifying our scientific and religious knowledge to be practical wisdom in and through mutual self-criticism and self-transformation—as opposed to a metaphysical theory, a phenomenological parallelism, or technical knowledge.[30] The matter of how to transform new scientific knowledge and technology into the wisdom of life in the "socio-cosmic" network of sociological and ecological relationships becomes the central issue at hand for interreligious and interdisciplinary dialogue between the sciences and religions, that is, the trilogue among sciences, theologies, and Asian religions.[31] That is to say, a *koan* (an evocative question) for the trilogue is how we may cultivate newly acquired knowledge from the natural sciences into useful wisdom for attaining new cosmic humanity—wisdom that may enable us to fully embody the tao of life into the sociocosmic web of the universe, transcending the uncontrollable greed of commercialism and unlimited selfish desires for convenience. Without doubt, this koan refers to spirituality.

The Content: Some Preliminary Suggestions

By adding the insights of interreligious dialogue and Asian religions, a trilogue of humility enables the dialogue between the sciences and religions to progress beyond its current limitations within the Western Christian framework and to embrace the real, pluri-religious world.[32] Some of my preliminary suggestions for future studies are as follows:

1. The primary locus for the dialogue between the sciences and religions should not be concerned with theoretical metaphysics (knowledge) but about the tao (way) of life (wisdom) in the common quest for a new cosmic humanity through mutual self-transformation, that is, self-cultivation and sanctification. The distinction between *inter*religious dialogue and *intra*religious dialogue is also helpful here for the science and religion dialogue (R. Panikkar).[33] The primary purpose of dialogue is neither to do apologetics for one's hypothesis, theory, or system of thought, nor to proselytize dialogue partners, but for mutual learning and growth through self-criticism, cross-examination, and self-transformation ("a humble approach").

2. The East Asian notions of nothingness, vacuity, and emptiness are worth serious consideration for the science and religion dialogue, as the reality of Non-Being becomes plausible in both the new physics and Christian theology.[34] The conception of God as the "Absolute Nothingness" might constitute a more promising theological strategy than the notion of *kenosis*—an inevitable logical consequence of the conservative doctrines of a personal God and divine omnipotence—in addressing the problem of theodicy (i.e., from Non-Being to Being vs. from Being to Non-Being). When criticizing scientific materialism, theologians in the science and religion dialogue seem unable to rid themselves of the old habits of essentialism and substantialism, a plausible basis for materialism. Process theology's alternative strategy of "becoming" also seems unsatisfactory because its core is unavoidably associated with a metaphysical dualism ("the bipolar God") of being ("entity"). A contemplation of nothingness would thus appear a welcome alternative in addressing this fundamental dilemma of the modern, Western mode of theological thinking (cf. the apophatic tradition of Christian spirituality and the negative theology of *via negativa*).[35]

3. The traditional Christian notion of linear time and the supremacy of time, still prominent in the dialogue between theology and science (i.e., "*when* science meets religion"), should be scrutinized in the light of the new physics and East Asian religious ideas that underscore the significance of space.[36] The logic of causality in Western thought, also still prevalent in the dialogue, should, in addition, be reevaluated in light of the possibility

of "synchronicity," a conceptual foundation of East Asian thought, I-Ching. Carl Jung, for example, stated suggestively: "Synchronicity takes the coincidence of events in space and time as meaning something more than mere chance, namely, a peculiar interdependence of objective events among themselves as well as the subjective (psychic) states of the observer or observers."[37]

4. The traditional Christian (or Greek) understanding of the term "nature," in common usage in the science and religion dialogue, is problematic because it cannot avoid the pejorative connotation inherited by the hierarchical dualism between the supernatural and the natural. The notion of kenosis (self-emptying) is a helpful, but unsatisfactory alternative since it still retains vestiges of dualism and a certain ambiguity of definition. In light of such considerations, it is worth taking into account the profound Taoist insights of nature and *wu-wei* (cf. "let it be itself").[38] The Chinese interpretation of nature bears the connotation of "self-so," "spontaneity," or "naturalness;" that is ,"the effective modality of the system that informs the actions of the agents that compose it."[39] In other words, "nature" in East Asian thought is the primary "self-so" (natural) manifestation of the Tao. In Chinese, natural science denotes self-so science: it does not refer to mere knowledge but wisdom. In the Bible, nature as God's creation is good, and the denial of its goodness as self-so was in fact a fallacy of Gnosticism. With such an enhanced clarification of the ambiguous English term "nature," the "theology of nature" would make more sense.

5. This self-so perspective calls for a fundamental change of attitude towards nature, from the paradigm of domination and control to that of participation and appropriateness. The Neo-Confucian paradigm of participation and appropriateness conceives of an organismic (organic + cosmic) wholeness in which everything is interconnected in the web of life. In this organismic universe, human beings are not construed as autonomous egos striving for transcendent self-determination in order to dominate, manipulate, and control nature, but rather as responsible participants, appropriately responding to the interconnected whole in harmony with the "theanthropocosmic" (*theos* + *anthropos* + *cosmos*) trajectory (the tao).[40] Within this framework, the issue is not how to control and engineer nature for maximum human benefit but a right discernment of, and respect for, the dynamic wholeness of the Nature.[41] The trilogue of humility (natural

sciences, Christian theologies, and Asian religions) so conceived, therefore, is not so much based on the strife (Western) model of dialectical dualism, but on the harmony (Eastern) model of dialogical (or trialogical) holism, as it metaphorically appears in the symbol of the Triune Great Ultimate (*T'ai-chi*).[42] The organismic holism that conceives of the triadic communion of heaven, Earth, and humanity as the foundation of cosmic diversity is ecologically more fitting. Furthermore, this Neo-Confucian vision is arguably more congruent with the findings of contemporary areas of scientific inquiry such as quantum physics, chaos theory, complex system, self-organization, information system, and so forth.[43] There is no doubt that this will be a fascinating topic for future discussion.

Notes

1. Philip Jenkins, *The Next Christendom: The Coming of Global Christianity* (Oxford: Oxford University Press, 2002), 16, 39–42.
2. Adrian Hastings, *The Church in Africa, 1450–1950* (Oxford: Clarendon, 1996), 485.
3. Jenkins, *The Next Christendom*, 79–105.
4. See W. Mark Richardson and Wesley J. Wildman, *Religion and Science: History, Method, Dialogue* (New York & London: Routledge, 1996), xi–xiii.
5. Eugene M. Klaaren, *Religious Origin of Modern Science: Belief in Creation in Seventeenth-Century Thought* (Grand Rapids: Eerdmans, 1977).
6. John Hedley Brooke, *Science and Religion: Some Historical Perspectives* (Cambridge: Cambridge University Press, 1991), 52–81.
7. See Michael Ruse, *A Darwinian Evolutionist's Philosophy* (Seoul: Acanet, 2004).
8. John Polkinghorne, *Belief in God in an Age of Science* (New Haven: Yale University Press, 1998), 112–13.
9. Wilfred Cantwell Smith, "The Christian in a Religiously Plural World," in *Christianity and Other Religions*, ed. John Hick and Brian Hebblethwaite (Philadelphia: Fortress Press, 1980), 91.
10. Scott W. Sunquist, ed., *A Dictionary of Asian Christianity* (Grand Rapids: Eerdmans, 2001), 703, 703–5. Also see Jacques Gernet, *China and the Christian Impact: A Conflict of Culture*, trans. Janet Lloyd (Cambridge: Cambridge University Press, 1985), 20–22, 57–63.
11. See *Proceedings of the Congress of Asian Theologians (CATS), 25 May–1 June 1997, Suwon, Korea*, ed. Dhyanchand Carr and Philip Wickeri (Hong Kong: Continuation Committee of the Congress of Asian Theologians, 1997–98).
12. Daniel S. Thiagarajah and A. Wati Longchar, eds., *Visioning New Life Together among Asian Resources: The Third Congress of Asian Theologians* (Hong Kong: CCA, 2002), 294–95.

13. Ian G. Barbour, *Religion and Science: Historical and Contemporary Issues* (San Francisco: HarperSanFrancisco, 1997), 80.
14. See John Polkinghorne, *The Faith of a Physicist: Reflections of a Bottom-Up Thinker* (Minneapolis: Fortress Press, 1996).
15. Thiagarajah, *Visioning*, 294.
16. Aloysius Pieris, *Love Meets Wisdom: A Christian Experience of Buddhism* (Maryknoll, N.Y.: Orbis Books, 1988), 3.
17. See Robert Cummings Neville, *Boston Confucianism: Portable Tradition in the Late-Modern World* (Albany: State University of New York Press, 2000); Diana L. Eck, *A New Religious America: How a "Christian Country" Has Now Become the World's Most Religiously Diverse Nation* (San Francisco: HarperSanFrancisco, 2001).
18. David Tracy, *Dialogue with the Other: The Inter-Religious Dialogue* (Louvain: Peeters Press, 1990), 95.
19. Diana L. Eck, *Encountering God: A Spiritual Journey from Bozeman to Banras* (Boston: Beacon Press, 1993), x.
20. Heup Young Kim, *Wang Yang-ming and Karl Barth: A Confucian-Christian Dialogue* (Lanham, Md.: University Press of America, 1996), esp. 139–41.
21. Korean Neo-Confucianism emphasizes the attitude of respect or reverence. See Heup Young Kim, *Christ and the Tao* (Hong Kong: Christian Conference of Asia, 2003), 111–16.
22. Alfred N. Whitehead, *Science and the Modern World* (New York: Macmillan, 1967), esp. chap. 2.
23. See David Lochhead, *The Dialogical Imperative: A Christian Reflection on Interfaith Encounter* (Maryknoll, N.Y.: Orbis, 1988), 40–45.
24. John Marks Templeton, *The Humble Approach: Scientists Discover God* (Philadelphia and London: Templeton Foundation Press, 1995), 167.
25. See Edward W. Said, *Orientalism* (New York: Vintage Books, 1979); Bill Aschcroft, Gareth Griffiths, and Helen Tiffin, eds., *The Post-Colonial Studies Reader* (London and New York: Routledge, 1995).
26. See Hans-Georg Gadamer, *Truth and Method*, 2nd ed., trans. Joel Weinsheimer and Donald G. Marshall (New York: Crossroad, 1989).
27. Tao is an inclusive term, widely used in East Asian religions, with various connotations. For example, "Tao is a Way, a path, a road, and by common metaphorical extension it becomes in ancient China the right Way of life, the Way of governing, the ideal Way of human existence, the Way of the Cosmos, the generative-normative Way (Pattern, path, course) of existence as such" (Herbert Fingarette, *Confucius—The Secular as Sacred* [New York: Harper & Row, 1972], 19).
28. Hans Küng and Julia Ching, *Christianity and Chinese Religions*, trans. Peter Beyer (New York: Doubleday, 1989), xii–xiii. It is noteworthy that Confucianism and Taoism are not merely of Chinese religions but of East Asian religions, just as Christianity is not only a Palestine religion.
29. See Kim, *Wang Yang-ming and Karl Barth*, 33–36, 171–74.
30. The Neo-Confucian doctrine of the unity of knowledge and action refutes the dualism of knowledge and practice, but insists on their ontological unity (see ibid., 29–32). Cf. Daniel Hardy, "The God Who Is with the World," in *Science Meets Faith*, ed. F. Watts (London: SPCK, 1998), 136–37.

31. Kim, *Christ and the Tao*, 142–48. I proposed the tao paradigm of theology (*theo-tao*) to overcome the dualism in contemporary Christian theology between the logos paradigm (*theo-logos*; in the religion-and-science dialogue, a metaphysical theology) and the praxis paradigm (*theo-praxis*; an ecological ethics); see ibid., 135–54, 155–82.
32. Christopher Southgate et al., *God, Humanity and the Cosmos: A Textbook in Science and Religion* (Edinburgh: T & T Clark, 1999), 230–31.
33. See R. Panikkar, *The Intrareligious Dialogue* (New York and Ramsey: Paulist Press, 1978).
34. See Fritzof Capra, *The Tao of Physics: An Exploration of the Parables Between Modern Physics and Eastern Mysticism*, 2nd ed. (Boston: Shambhala, 1983), esp. 208–23.
35. See Heup Young Kim, "The Word Made Flesh: A Korean Perspective on Ryu Youngmo's Christotao," in *One Gospel—Many Cultures: Case Studies and Reflection on Cross-Cultural Theology*, ed. Mercy Amba Oduyoye and Hendrik M. Vroom (Amsterdam: Rodopi, 2003), 143–44; also, Kim, *Christ & the Tao*, 167–72.
36. Cf. Ian Barbour, *When Science Meets Religion: Enemies, Strangers, or Partners?* (San Francisco: HarperSanFrancisco, 2002).
37. C. G. Jung, "Foreword," in *The I Ching or Book of Changes*, 3rd ed., trans. Richard Wilhelm (Princeton, NJ: Princeton University Press, 1967), xxiv; also see xxi–xxix.
38. Barbour, *When Science Meets Religion*, 113. Also see Southgate et al., *God, Humanity, and the Cosmos*, 233–35; Jürgen Moltmann, *God in Creation*, trans. M. Kohl (London: SCM, 1985), 87–88; Moltmann, *Science and Wisdom*, trans. M. Kohl (London: SCM, 2003), chap. 12.
39. Michael C. Kalton, "Asian Religious Tradition and Natural Science: Potentials, Present and Future," unpublished paper, the CTNS Korea Religion & Science Workshop, Seoul, January 18–22, 2002.
40. See Kim, *Wang Yang-ming and Karl Barth*, 175-88; Kim, *Christ and the Tao*, 155–76.
41. See Heup Young Kim, "A Tao of Interreligious dialogue in an Age of Globalization: An East Asian Christian Perspective," *Political Theology* 6, no. 4 (2005): 503–16.
42. See Heup Young Kim, "Life, Ecology, and Theo-tao: Towards an Ecumenism of the Theanthropocosmic Tao," in *Windows into Ecumenism: Essays in Honor of Ahn Jae Woong* (Hong Kong: Christian Conference of Asia, 2005), 143–46. Also Shu-hsien Liu and Robert E. Allinson, *Harmony and Strife: Contemporary Perspectives, East and West* (Hong Kong: Chinese University Press, 1988).
43. Cf. Fritzof Capra, *The Tao of Physics*; Capra, *The Web of Life: A New Scientific Understanding of Living System* (London: Flamingo/Harper Collins, 1996).

Conclusion

SCIENCE, RELIGION, AND THE FUTURE OF DIALOGUE

RONALD COLE-TURNER

THE INCREASED RELIGIOUS CONFLICT that has so far marred the opening decade of the new millennium makes the choice for dialogue more urgent and yet more difficult. It is more urgent, of course, for in dialogue we find some hope that we might avoid the much-prophesied "clash of civilizations," with the prospect of enduring hostility and violence. But it is also more difficult, not just because of growing distrust but most of all because of growing complexity of the conversation. Anyone who still divides the cultural world between science and religion is plainly ignoring both history and the subtleties of the present. Science and religion interact today in complex ways, usually but not always with positive results. And anyone who thinks that in the wake of the cold war, the global geopolitical tension is defined simply as a struggle between Christendom and its remnants in the West and a monolithic Islam is blissfully ignorant of the internal conflicts that distress the inner circles of the world's great faiths.

The contributors to this volume agree on taking the path of dialogue, believing that science and religion each have something of value to offer to each other and to humanity as a whole. For us and for the newly formed International Society for Science and Religion (ISSR), the dialogue is defined by two axes of relationship. The first, of course, is between the various natural sciences and religion, while the second line of relationship is within the various religions themselves as each one struggles internally with the best way to engage the sciences. So the dialogue we seek is new in many respects. It does not move between two fixed poles—science and religion—but around dynamic and changing realities, emerging dichotomies, and tentative alliances. Chastened by recent events, it is nonetheless a dialogue that clings to the hope that by engaging one another at the deepest level of our beliefs and yearnings, we can understand and respect both our differences and our common humanity.

The Multiple Dialogues of Science and Religion

It is not uncommon today to find adherents of various traditions living next door to each other, usually in harmony. Equally true is the sad fact that, sometimes, followers of one faith divide among themselves. At stake, at least some of the time, is the right way to engage science. These divisions can harden in opposition, sometimes with contempt if not violence against fellow believers. In such a world, the dialogue between science and religion is often first of all a conversation within a religion itself about its attitudes toward science.

While each faith tradition is unique, it is not uncommon to find in each a traditional and a progressive wing, often spread across a range of suboptions. At one end of the spectrum of persons with religious commitments are those who see religion as valuable because it *is* tradition, an anchor against social and cultural change, a source of absolute commitment in a world of ideas that shift with time and values that adjust to fashion. For them, to accommodate religion to modernity is to destroy what makes it religion. At the other end of the spectrum are those who see religious traditions merely as starting points, as posing the great perennial questions but having nothing of value left to offer as answers. In between, where most people of religious commitment actually live, stands a wide range of positions with more or less value placed on traditional texts, beliefs, or observances and more or less willingness to reform some dimension of tradition in light of new knowledge from the sciences, among other sources.

Traditionalists of one faith may have less in common with some in their own faith than with the traditionalists of a completely different faith tradition. For example, Christians who advocate a theological and conceptual openness to science often find themselves joining like-minded individuals of other faiths as they both square off against the more traditional followers of their own faith. At the same time, the pseudoscientific movement known as "intelligent design," oddly popular with traditional

Christians in America, is becoming popular with traditional Muslims in Asia. Diverging attitudes toward tradition and modernity split the religions not from each other but internally, each against their own along fault lines of progressive vs. traditionalist. The same phenomenon then joins the like-minded of various faiths in a new, albeit limited, consensus.

So we must ask whether the global "clash of civilizations" is between religions or between two religious views of science. Of course, arguing that it is nothing but an internal religious conflict is to reduce the complexity of our situation to yet another false simplicity. The world's religions, with all their internal conflicts and debates, are an exasperating mix, all the more so because of the intellectual challenges posed by the natural sciences and the transformative potentials of technology. What is needed is not a two-way conversation so much as a multifaceted exploration, prompted by the ever-changing insights of the natural sciences and the new creations of technology as these provoke new insights among the faiths, each in intramural and extramural conversation with each other. Their dialogue with science, dynamic and transformative, promises to reenergize their interaction with each other.

As individuals in the various faith traditions engage the natural sciences and the expanding fields of technology, they ask remarkably similar questions. Of course, each tradition draws upon its own mode of argument and its own distinctive resources and concepts. But how people of faith honor and respect their tradition in the face of intellectual and technological challenge is a question in common across the faiths, and learning how each tradition comes to terms with the polarity of tradition and modernity is mutually rewarding. In one respect, this is a question of method in theology or religion. How does theology or critical reflection upon religion decide about the relative virtues of conflicting interpretations of the same religious tradition? How does it balance claims not just of ancient scripture and subsequent authoritative texts that interpret these scriptures, but the new intellectual claims that arise from well-founded insights of science? Each world faith has among its followers people who hold to a range of theological methods, and there is much to gain in the sorting out and clarifying of these methods by sharing across faith communities. The way any one faith responds to science is potentially illuminating for other faiths.

Beyond method, however, are questions of substance, such as how religious cosmologies engage their contemporary scientific counterparts, or how religious views of the living things or human nature are challenged and informed by biology. The interplay between religion, physics, and cosmology is nicely explored by the other contributors to this volume. Other writers have begun to probe the impact of biology, evolution, and genetics on religious views of life and humanity.[1] As research in evolution moves forward, fueled in part by genetics and the ability to compare genes and whole genomes across the entire spectrum of life, biology stands on the threshold of rich and detailed new insight into the emergence of life, here and perhaps on other planets. Questions of purpose in evolution can be posed in new ways.[2] This research might open up promising new forms of religious engagement that avoid the sterile impasse of creationism. In particular, a renewed theological reflection on evolution could bring a new and profound understanding of creation.

What Lies Ahead for Science and Religion?

There can be no doubt that these questions will receive much more attention in the future, in the ISSR and beyond. At the same time, the dialogue between science and religion has room for growth in new directions that have received little or no attention so far. New challenges arise not just from the changing political and cultural context of globalization but also because of the explosion of technology as a global force. Organizations such as the International Society can play a key role in challenging excessive traditionalism in all the religions or by calling into question certain movements, such as intelligent design, that confuse the public and distort the relationship that might exist between science and religion.

One might hope that as religion and science engage each other in more public venues and across a widening array of subjects, those individuals with advanced theological training will take greater note of the dialogue and will take up in a systematic way the task of constructive theological interpretation of recent science. The result could be a rich and comprehensive new theology of nature, building upon the achievements of the past decades but going far beyond them in laying out the theological visions they inspire. Such work will likely begin in academic circles but will have the potential to radiate outward into wider circles, shaping the views of the adherents of the religions and affecting their interpretations of science. If successful, this effort will build strong public support for research in every field of science, from cosmology and space exploration to molecular and developmental biology. But in the absence of such an effort, we can expect that religious followers will be unable to find religious value in science and that they will fall prey to accepting false dichotomies such as creation versus evolution.

Furthermore, any theology that has not engaged science and allowed itself to be enriched and expanded in the encounter is not prepared to take up the task of understanding and responding to technology. At stake here is not just the point that individuals, religious or not, need to know something about recent science in order to understand technology. For instance, lack of knowledge of biology and genetics leaves one vulnerable to misinterpretations and distortions about biotechnology and, at the same time, unable to think seriously about the real concerns it does raise. Our point, however, goes beyond the necessary knowledge base out of which individuals, religious or not, comprehend and engage increasingly complex technologies. It is religion as systems of thought, and not just the individual followers, that must be engaged by science and take the implications of science into account. Religious ways of thinking, their structures of belief and their theological concepts, must be informed by the encounter with science and come away changed and enriched. Just as an individual cannot adequately respond to the challenges of biotechnology without knowing something about biology, genetics, and evolution, so a theology cannot comment as a theology without having first encountered the science and having incorporated it into its own theological understanding of nature. A theology that today asserts the unique and recent creation of *homo sapiens* (which virtually everyone accepted two hundred years ago) cannot adequately or fairly assess a biotechnology that moves human genes to other organisms, much less takes us into the ever more audacious pathways of biotechnological transformations.

Indeed, the sheer creative dynamism of new and emerging technology poses the most urgent and difficult challenges for the science and religion dialogue. The challenge is one of ethics: how should we use these new technologies and how far should we go in permitting their development? But the intellectual challenge is far deeper than an ethical assessment of yes, no, or how far. It is based upon and includes a theological encounter with the underlying science, a point that has just been noted. But as important as that is, it is only the prerequisite for the greater work that lies ahead. The deeper challenge, already clearly in view and yet so often overlooked, has to do with the meaning of the technology itself and the new realities it creates.

It is inadequate to think that science seeks to understand nature and that technology merely puts that understanding to work in useful ways. While this approach is no doubt true to some extent, such an assessment misses the core dynamic of technology as the power to create what does not yet exist, and in so doing to change at least at some level the laws of nature. If science seeks to understand nature, technology creates novel forms of nature that cry out for understanding. Consider the familiar example of cloning or somatic cell nuclear transfer. The basic law of nature, understood by biology and fundamental to our commonsense view of life and thus to religion, is that life develops from embryo to fetus to child to adult. In complex organisms such as mammals, the process goes forward, not backward, until the advent of mammalian cloning, a technology that reverses the direction of development and thereby brings something new into the natural world.

There are other examples, many of them more profound in their significance and potential consequences than cloning, even if the public is not nearly so engaged. Nanotechnology brings engineering to the scale of a few molecules, moving single atoms and creating novel structures with surprising and unexpected properties and features. Public interest is largely limited to looking for new financial investment opportunities, and almost no one in religious or theological circles has engaged these developments, and, if they have, such engagement is then usually limited to ethics and safety issues. Those issues are complex, to be sure, but not profound or particularly novel. Not being addressed, however, are basic religious questions of the human role in nature, particularly at such a basic and powerful level, or what it will mean for human beings to discover the novel properties that come from rearranging matter atom by atom. Engineering at a scale vastly smaller than a living cell makes it possible to create or modify the smallest components of cells. This opens the pathway to entirely new strategies for medicine and for the alteration of living cells, from single-celled organisms to the cells in the human brain.

Indeed, it is the combination of nanotechnology with the revolution in molecular biology that is opening a new field sometimes called "synthetic biology," an umbrella term to describe a range of engineering strategies. One approach is to attempt to "recreate in unnatural chemical systems the emergent properties of living systems, including inheritance, genetics and evolution."[3] The other broad category of synthetic biology research is to "extract from living systems interchangeable parts that might be tested, validated as construction units, and reassembled to create devices that might (or might not) have analogues in living systems."[4] If the first approach makes inorganic components function as organic, the second makes organic components function as inorganic or in entirely different organic settings.

Organic molecules including DNA are being used to solve engineering problems, and inorganic molecules and structures are being integrated into organic systems so that the result is hard to classify. In either case, any line between organic and inorganic is blurred, along with religious or moral distinctions grounded upon that distinction. The novelty of the synthetic biology program is not just greater power and precision, although it is of course these things. The central feature of the novelty we encounter here is that the chemical structures of life are being revised in fundamental ways, with unknown limits and consequences, and in ways that blur the venerable distinction between organic and inorganic, living and nonliving.

Other research is under way to create minimal organisms, the simplest possible in terms of the number of genes and proteins. Some researchers are pursuing this goal by starting with the simplest naturally occurring organism and systematically removing genes in order to remove all that are not essential to life. Others are hoping to use DNA sequencing machines to create artificial chromosomes housing synthetic genes, thereby creating never-before-existing organisms *de novo*. The hope is that these minimized organisms will have a range of functions, from environmental to medical, because they will be more efficient than "natural life" in absorbing new genes and in avoiding mutation. If a synthesized structure is capable of functioning as a living cell and of replicating, will human beings have created life?

In a completely different context, the distinction (if there is one) between organic and inorganic and between natural and artifactual has emerged in one of the most intense public moral debates, that over the appropriateness of human embryo research. Some who oppose the use of human embryos in research have recently proposed that by using an altered form of nuclear transfer (commonly called "cloning"), it might be possible to create an entity that has the medical usefulness of a cloned embryo but lacks any possibility of developmental potential.[5] The alteration that precedes the nuclear transfer would assure that the resulting entity cannot develop as an embryo. Because it is an artifact and because it lacks potential, it is not an embryo and therefore may be used without moral qualms, or so the advocates of this strategy claim. The debate is further complicated by the fact that in all likelihood, all human or primate cloned "embryos" lack developmental potential, at least when created by today's nuclear transfer technology. Therefore, by the same logic, they too should not be regarded as embryos, something that advocates of altered nuclear transfer are probably not likely to concede. Here again, technology creates new entities that are hard to classify (embryo or nonembyro?). More precisely in this case, at least as of mid-2006, technology only promises to create these new entities, but even the promise triggers complex political maneuvering and moral debate.[6]

Another area of research undertaken only recently is to implant human embryonic stem cells into the early-stage fetus of rats or mice, in particular in the brain. This results in animals with functioning "human" cells. These "chimeras," as they are now being called, raise objections from anyone who believes there are clear species boundaries and that such boundaries must be respected absolutely in research, particularly when human beings are involved. For scientists, notions of species boundaries are quaint, and creating human-mouse chimeras is not fundamentally objectionable, at least according to a recent statement published in *Science*: "We unanimously rejected ethical objections grounded on unnaturalness or crossing species boundaries. Whether it is possible to draw a meaningful distinction between the natural and the unnatural is a matter of dispute."[7] Some religious people, especially those with traditional views of creation, will surely disagree. Whether theologians committed to science and religion dialogue will agree with the scientists or with their cobelievers remains to be seen. What is clear is that religiously or theologically enriched ethics needs to take up these questions for careful analysis and debate before research moves ahead.

Nowhere are these issues more urgent or the stakes higher than in the growing debate over the technological modification of human beings themselves. Advocates, sometimes calling themselves "transhumanists" or "posthumanists," argue that human beings should be free to develop and use a wide range of technologies to modify or enhance normal human traits in themselves and, with some limits, in their offspring. Some argue that the technologies for really successful human improvement are largely pursued in an incoherent way that fails to take full advantage of advances in one field to accelerate advances elsewhere, and thus they call for government support and high-level coordination of these efforts.[8] To date, there has been almost no attempt by religious scholars to engage these proposals, much less to reflect critically on their assumptions and aims, the most notable exception being a recent book by Brent Waters.[9]

The posthuman prospect deserves more sustained and serious attention. It raises a host of questions, such as whether we can "improve" ourselves technologically without destroying ourselves. More fundamentally it forces us to ask about ourselves and whether we have a nature that can or should be modified. Even more, it raises the question of our future and whether there can or should be a future beyond our current evolved status as a species. In relation to these questions, how are we to think about a creator who may even use technology as a new mode of creativity? Here, more urgently than anywhere else, we confront the extraordinary power of technology to create (or perhaps only promise to create) something new, in this case a species with human traits taken to a superhuman level. These questions are as theological as they are technological. Faced with such questions about our future as a species, old divisions and conflicts must be set aside so that we can struggle not with each other, but with the direction and the meaning of the new world we are about to create.

Notes

1. See, for example, the work of Arthur R. Peacocke, including *Theology for a Scientific Age: Being and Becoming—Natural, Divine and Human* (Minneapolis: Fortress Press, 1993).

2. Helpful in this regard is Simon Conway Morris, *Life's Solution: Inevitable Humans in a Lonely Universe* (Cambridge: Cambridge University Press, 2003).
3. See, for example, Steven A. Benner and A. Michael Sismour, "Synthetic Biology," *Nature Review Genetics* 6 (2005): 533–43, at 533.
4. Ibid., 533.
5. For a discussion of this and similar strategies, see the President's Council on Bioethics, *White Paper: Alternative Sources of Pluripotent Stem Cells* (Washington, D.C.: 2005).
6. In 2005, researchers in South Korea claimed success in producing human cloned embryos, but this claim has been withdrawn.
7. M. Greene, K. Schill, S. Takahashi, A. Bateman-House, T. Beauchamp, H. Bok, D. Cheney, J. Coyle, T. Deacon, D. Dennett, P. Donovan, O. Flanagan, S. Goldman, H. Greely, L. Martin, E. Miller, D. Mueller, A. Siegel, D. Solter, J. Gearhart, G. McKhann, and R. Faden, "Ethics: Moral Issues of Human-Non-Human Primate Neural Grafting," *Science* 309 (2005): 385–86.
8. See, for example, Mihail C. Roco and William Sims Bainbridge, eds., *Converging Technologies for Improving Human Performance: Nanotechnology, Biotechnology, Information Technology, and Cognitive Science* (Arlington, Va.: National Science Foundation, 2002).
9. Brent Waters, *From Human to Posthuman: Christian Theology and Technology in a Postmodern World* (Aldershot, England: Ashgate, 2006); see also *Journal of Evolution and Technology* 14, no. 2 (August 2005), devoted to "Religion and Transhumanism."

Contributors

Munawar A. Anees is a highly respected and renowned author on the subject of Islam and science. One of his books, *Islam and Biological Futures*, remains a pioneering classic. He is among the advisory editors of the *Journal of Islamic Science* and *Journal of Islamic Philosophy*.

Philip Clayton is Ingraham Professor at the Claremont School of Theology and professor of philosophy and religion at the Claremont Graduate University. He is the author or editor of over a dozen books, including *The Problem of God in Modern Thought*; *God and Contemporary Science*; *In Whom We Live and Move and Have Our Being*; *The Oxford Handbook of Religion and Science*; and *Mind and Emergence: From Quantum to Consciousness*.

Ronald Cole-Turner is H. Parker Sharp Chair of Theology and Ethics at Pittsburgh Theological Seminary. His research focuses on genetics and biotechnology, particularly as they affect the meaning and future of human life. He is the author and editor of books including, *The New Genesis*; *Pastoral Genetics*; *Human Cloning: Religious Responses*; *Beyond Cloning*; and *God and the Embryo* and has written numerous articles and chapters in books.

George F. R. Ellis is a professor of applied mathematics at the University of Cape Town. He is a Fellow of the Royal Astronomical Society and the Institute of Mathematics and Its Applications. The many prizes he has been awarded include the Star of South Africa Medal, which was presented to him in 1999 by President Nelson Mandela. Coauthor with Stephen W. Hawking of *The Large Scale Structure of Space Time* (1973), he has also written more than two hundred scientific papers and eight major books.

Carl Feit is Dr. Joseph and Rachel Ades Chair in Health Sciences, associate professor of biology, and chairperson of the Science Division of Yeshiva College. Dr. Feit came to the Biology Department of Yeshiva College in 1985 from the Laboratory for Immunodiagnosis at the Sloan-Kettering Institute for Cancer Research. Dr. Feit received his Ph.D. in microbiology and immunology from Rutgers University. He is a founding member of the International Society for Science and Religion and serves on its Executive Committee. Dr. Feit is also an ordained rabbi and a Talmudic scholar who has lectured on Talmud and taught Talmud classes for many years.

Heup Young Kim is professor of systematic theology and a former dean of the College of Humanities and Liberal Arts, the Graduate School of Theology, and University Chapel at Kangnam University, Korea. He holds a BSE from Seoul National University, M.Div. and Th.M. from Princeton Theological Seminary, and a Ph.D. from Graduate Theological Union; he was also a fellow at the Harvard Center for the Study of World Religions, GTU Center for Theology and the National Sciences, and Cambridge Centre for Advanced Religious and Theological Studies. He has published numerous works in the areas of interfaith dialogue, theology of religions, Asian theology, and theology and science, in both English and Korean.

John Polkinghorne is an Anglican priest, past president of Queens' College, Cambridge University, and former professor of mathematical physics at Cambridge. Polkinghorne resigned his chair in physics to study for the Anglican priesthood. After completing his theological studies and serving at parishes, he returned to Cambridge. He is the author of a series of books on the compatibility of religion and science. In 1997, Polkinghorne was knighted by Queen Elizabeth II for distinguished service to science, religion, learning, and medical ethics. He was the recipient of the 2002 Templeton Prize.

Holmes Rolston III is University Distinguished Professor and professor of philosophy at Colorado State University. He has written seven books, most recently *Genes, Genesis and God*; *Science and Religion: A Critical Survey*; *Philosophy Gone Wild*; *Environmental Ethics*; and *Conserving*

Natural Value. He has lectured on all seven continents. He gave the Gifford Lectures, University of Edinburgh, 1997–1998. He received the Templeton Prize in Religion in 2003, given by Prince Philip in Buckingham Palace.

B. V. Subbarayappa is an Honorary Professor at the National Institute of Advanced Studies in Bangalore. He was formerly executive secretary of the Indian National Science Academy in New Delhi and the project coordinator and member secretary of the National Commission for the History of Science in India as well as the director of the Discovery of India Project, at the Nehru Centre in Bombay. He was the president of the Science Division of the International Union of History and Philosophy of Science (1997–2001), which is related to UNESCO. He is also the recipient of an honorary doctorate from the University of Bologna (Italy).

Trinh Xuan Thuan is a professor of astronomy at the University of Virginia. He studies galaxy formation and evolution. He has written several books for the general public, including *The Quantum and the Lotus*, where he explores with the French Buddhist monk Matthieu Ricard the many remarkable connections between the ancient teachings of Buddhism and the findings of modern science.

Fraser Watts is reader in theology and science at the University of Cambridge, and a Fellow of Queens' College. He was previously a clinical psychologist with the UK Medical Research Council and has been president of the British Psychological Society. He works on the interface of psychology and theology, and directs the Psychology and Religion Research Group at the University of Cambridge.

Index

Abrahamic traditions
  based on the land ethic, 36–37
  in the dialogue, 63
  a model for the dialogue, 67–70
Absolute Nothingness, 129
absolute truth, 3, 60, 115
absolutism
  damage of, 70
  in the dialogue, 126
  in Hinduism, 92
abstinence (*yama*), 97
aesthetics and science, 18
al-Bīrūmī, 93
al-Khwārizmī, 93
Anees, Munawar A., viii, 81–89, 145
anthropic principle, 5, 45, 112–13
apologia
  in Christian missions to Asia, 123–24
  in the dialogue, 126
  Muslim, on modernity, 85–87
apophatic theology, 44
arrogance in religion, 60
artha (value-based living), 92–93
āsana (yoga postures), 98
Asian Christianity and science, 121–33
  bridge building myth, 122–23
  issues for dialogue, 128–31
  pluralism, 124–25
  the trilogue model, 125–28
Aspect, Alain, 108
astronomy in the Vedic period, 92, 93
autonomous effectiveness of the mind, 15
autonomous existence, 107
Ayurvedic medicine, 92

bad, measuring, 16
balance with nature (*loka-puruṣa-sāmya*), 92
Barbour, Ian, 75, 124
beauty, rational, as evidence of a creator, 30
behaviorists. *See* neobehaviorists
believers and scientists, 66
Bell, John, 108
Bell's inequality, 108
bhakti mārga (divine devotion), 92
biobibliographies, origin of, 83
biographical dictionaries, origin of, 83
biological sciences compared with Buddhist impermanence, 105
biology, synthetic, 141
Bohr, Niels, 111–12
book burning, 84
brain's influence on development, 10–11
breath control (*pranāyāma*), 98
bridge building metaphor, 122–23
Brooke, John, 122
Bucaille, Maurice, 85–86
Buddhism and science, 101–19
  Buddhism as a science, 103
  convergent views, 117–18
  emptiness, 110–12
  a Great Watchmaker?, 112–16
  grounds for a dialogue, 101–04
  impermanence, 104–06
  interdependence, 106–10

cancer to creativity analogy, 46
CATS (Congress of Asian Theologians), 123–24
causal effectiveness, 12–15
causality
  in biology, 56
  in Buddhism, 106–07, 115
  mutual, 106
  in physics, 12–16
  predictability compared, 46
  time and, 129–30
chance, to explain the nature of the universe, 6, 113–14
chaos theory and predictability, 46
chess and the Martians analogy, 13
chimeras, 142–43
choice and the nature of humanity, 8
Christian missions to Asia, 123–24
Christianity
  context for the dialogue, 60
  the damage of absolutism, 70
  motivations for dialogue, 69–70
  politicized interpretation, 64
  secularization of, 57–58
Civilization of the Book, 84
Clayton, Philip, viii, 63–71, 145
cloning, 142
cognition and consciousness, 9–10
Cole-Turner, Ronald, viii, 135–43, 145
colonialism of Western Christianity, 123
complexity theory, 49–50
concentration (*dhārana*), 98
concentration, prolonged (*dhyāna*), 98
Congress of Asian Theologians (CATS), 123–24
consciousness
  cognition and, 9–10
  matter and, 116
  studies of, 50–51
consilience of science and religion, 22
consumption as a disease, 34
contingency's influence on science, 54
Convivencia, 84
Copenhagen interpretation of quantum theory, 111–12
corruption and power, 34
Cosmic Background Radiation, 15
cosmological constant, 6
cosmology
  Buddhist impermanence compared, 104–05
  Buddhist interdependence and, 109–10
  Buddhist view, 115–16
  and the nature of the universe, 5–8
Counterbalance Foundation, 65
"creation" of knowledge, 83
creationism, 138–39
creativity, cancer analogy, 46
creator
  in Buddhism, 114–15
  in Christianity, 30, 44–48
  to explain the nature of the universe, 6–8
  in Hinduism, 94
  in Islam, 82, 88
  in Judiasm, 76
cruciform creation, 36
cultural imperialism of Western Christianity, 123
cultural insensitivity, damage of, 63–64
cultural neutrality of science, 54, 56
culture
  contextual influence on religion, 57–59
  contextual influence on science, 54–57
  how to value it, 33–34

influence on science in India, 94
variety, 47
cyclical universe, 115–16

Darwinism
in Asian Christianity, 122
in Buddhism, 117
early responses to, 45–46
social, 17
on survival, 35
decimal system, 93
deep ethics, 20, 129, 130
delusion, 106
Dennett, Daniel C., 9–10
Descartes, René, 116
descriptive-comparative stage of the dialogue, 125–26
design, to explain the nature of the universe, 6–7
designation and interdependence, 107
detached desire (*kāma*), 93
determinism and the nature of humanity, 11–16
development, challenge of, 36
devotion (*bhakti mārga*), 92
dhārana (concentration), 98
dharma (right thinking and action), 92–93
dhyāna (prolonged concentration), 98
diachronic vs. synchronic understanding, 42–43
dialogue. *See* science and religion dialogue *and subsequent issues*
Dirac, Paul, 30
discernment, 21
dissipative systems, 49–50
distinctiveness, 59
divine providential action and scientific reliability, 46–47
dogmatism, 3–4, 123–24, 126
Donald, Merlin, 9–10
double identity, scientist and believer, 66
dualism
Buddhist view, 116
in the dialogue, 129, 130
EPR experiment, 108
mind-body, 97, 116
quantum theory, 111–12

Earth, future of, 36–37
ecumenical dialogue, importance of, 49
effectiveness, 12–15
Einstein, Albert, 107–09
electivity across religions, 57
Ellis, George F. R., vii, 3–25, 145
embryonic stem cells, 31
emotions, 18–19
emptiness, 110–12, 129
environment (nature), 36
environment (surroundings), 10–11
epiphenomenon, 9
epistemology compared with ontology, 20–21, 46
EPR experiment, 107–09
eschatology, 47
essentialism, 129
ethics
balanced with reason and emotion, 19
causal effectiveness of, 13–14
common to all religions, 23
in the dialogue, 139–40
invented or discovered?, 20
kenosis, 20, 129, 130
the metaquestion, 31
and moral realism, 20
and science, 16–18
value-based living, 92–93
Eurocentrism, 122
evil, 35–36

evolution
breadth of process, 45–46
in the dialogue, 138
and the possibility landscape, 15–16
evolutionary psychology, 17
existence and evidence of existence, 20–21
eyeglasses analogy, 14–15

faith, 18–19, 57
Feinstein, Moshe, 79
Feit, Carl, viii, 75–80, 146
Foucault, Léon, 109–10
Foucault's pendulum and Buddhist interdependence, 109–10
fundamentalism(s), 4, 20

genome's function in brain development, 10–11
geology compared with Buddhist impermanence, 105
Gisin, Nicolas, 108–09
Gnosticism and self-so, 130
God, unity of (*Tawhid*), 81
Golshani, Mehdi, 65
good, measuring, 16
Gould, Stephen Jay, 34
grandiosity, 59, 60
gross impermanence, 104

Halakha, 77–78
halakhic analysis compared with scientific methodology, 76–77
Heisenberg, Werner, 104, 111
Hinduism and science, 91–99
holistic approach compared with reductionism, 101
hope, 18–19
horizontal vs. vertical perspective, 47
"how?" and "why?," 28, 29
hubris, 3–4
human action (*kharma mārga*), 91–92
human mind, dualism of, 97, 116
humanity, nature of
in the dialogue, 5
neuroscience and, 8–11
physics and determinism, 11–16
humanization, 127–28
humility, 59–60, 125–26
Huxley, Julian, 97

Id (Freud), 54
identity as scientist and believer, 66
'ilm. *See* knowledge
imagination, 56
impermanence, 104–06
Indian religions, 91
inflationary era of the universe, 15
information, causal effectiveness of, 13
Inquisition, 84
intelligent beings, inevitability of, 6
intelligent design in religious factions, 136–37
intention, 14–15
interdependence, 106–10
International Society for Science and Religion (ISSR), vii, 32, 37, 41, 51, 99, 135
intuition compared with the scientific method, 101
investigation in science and Buddhism, 101–04
Iqra (read), 82
Islam and science, 81–89
"Islamic" science, 87–88
ISSR (International Society for Science and Religion), vii, 32, 37, 41, 51, 99, 135
"It," science encounters reality, 28, 42

Jenkins, Philip, 121
Jewish law, 77–78
jñāna- mārga. See knowledge
Journal of Islamic Science, 88
Judah the Prince, 78
Judaism and science, 75–80
judgment in science, 56
Jung, Carl, 130

kāma (detached desire), 93
Kant, Immanuel, 31
karma mārga (human action), 91–92
Karo, Yosef, 78
kataphatic utterance, 44
kenosis, 20, 129, 130. *See also* ethics
Khalifah, Rashad, 86
Kim, Heup Young, viii, 121–33, 146
knowledge
  in the dialogue, 129
  the Hindu view (*jñāna-margā*), 92
  the Islamic view (*'ilm*), 81–84
koan (question), 128
Küng, Hans, 127–28

land ethic in the Abrahamic traditions, 36–37
lawfulness in science, 54
life, 45, 112–13, 141–42
logical positivism in science, 59
loka-puruṣa-sāmya (balance), 92

Mach, Ernst, 110
Maimonides, Moses, 75–76
Martians and chess analogy, 13
materialism
  on the causal effectiveness of ethics, 14
  in the dialogue, 129
  inherent contradiction, 13
mathematical equations, beauty and significance, 30, 44–45
meaning and science, 18, 34
mechanism vs. relativism, 8–9
medicinal chemistry (*rasaśāstra*), 92, 93
mercy as knowledge, 82
metaphysics, 7, 18, 129
metaquestion, 29
the middle way, 106–07
mind-body dualism, 97, 116
Mishneh Torah, 76
Mitchell, Edgar, 37
modernity
  across religions, 136–37
  associated with the West, 56
  challenge to Muslim scholarship, 84–85
  explained, 54
  Islamic view, 85–87
mokśa (spiritual emancipation), 93
Monod, Jacques, 113
Moore, Keith, 86
moral realism and the nature of ethics, 28
multiverse, to explain the nature of the universe, 7–8, 114
Muslim Association for the Advancement of Science, 88
mutual causality, 106

Nagarjuna, 111, 115
Nagel, Thomas, 55
Nasr, Seyyed Hossein, 63, 87
natural selection and random variation, 15–16
nature
  in the dialogue, 130
  how to value it, 33
  view of religion, 23–24
nature vs. nurture, 10–11, 15–16
necessity, to explain the nature of the universe, 113–14
neobehaviorists and the mind, 9–10

neuroscience
  discoveries in this millenium, 50
  distinguished from physics, 12
  and the nature of humanity, 8–11
neutrality, cultural, of science, 54, 56
niyama (observance), 97
Non-Being, 129
nonlocality and Buddhist interdependence, 107–09
normative-constructive stage of the dialogue, 126
nothingness, 110–12, 129
nurture, nature vs., 10–11, 15–16

objectivity as a necessary struggle, 54–57
observance (*niyama*), 97
ontology compared with epistemology, 20–21, 46
oral (Jewish) law, 78
organismic holism, 130–31
original sin, 34, 54
"otherworldliness" and science in India, 94

peace, challenge of, 36
Penrose, R., 23
Perfection of Wisdom, 111
personal realm, 28
perspectives, religion and science compared, 23–24, 44, 47
physics
  Buddhist interdependence and, 107–10
  causal incompleteness, 14–16
  a delicate balance, 5–6
  impermanence in, 105–06
  and the nature of humanity, 11–16
Pieris, Aloysius, 124–25
pluralism in the Asian religious experience, 123–25
Podolsky, Boris, 107–09
Polanyi, Michael, 43–44
politicization of religion, 64
Polkinghorne, John, vii–viii, 27–32, 41–51, 124, 146
Popper, Karl, 60
population, challenge of, 36
possibility landscape, 15–16
posthumanism, 143
postures, yoga (*āsana*), 98
power and corruption, 34
practice, distinguished from religion, 57
pranāyāma (breath control), 98
pratyāhāra (sense withdrawal), 98
predictability compared with causality, 46
principle of complementarity, 111–12
process theology, 129
prolonged concentration (*dhyāna*), 98
psychology, evolutionary, 17

quantum theory
  Copenhagen interpretation, 111–12
  similarity to Buddhist interdependence, 107–09, 117–18
  on the unpredictable nature of physical processes, 46
question (*koan*), 128
quintessence, 6
Qur'anic literalism, 85–87

random variation and natural selection, 15–16
rasaśāstra (medicinal chemistry), 92
rational beauty, as evidence of a creator, 30, 44–45
rational transparency, as evidence of a creator, 30, 44–45
rationality, guided by values, 18, 19
read (*Iqra*), compelled by the Qur'an, 82

realia. *See* reality
realism, moral, 20
reality
  Buddhist view, 110–12
  disparate religious views, 48
  focus of Buddhist study, 102
  Jewish law and, 79–80
  "Thou" vs. "It," 28, 42
reason, balanced with emotion and ethics, 19
Reconquista, 84
reductionism
  on the causal effectiveness of ethics, 14
  holism compared, 101
  in Islam, 82
  limiting science, 56
Rees, M., 7
regionality, science and religion contrasted, 47–48
relative truth, 106, 115
relativism
  ethics and, 20
  vs. mechanism, 8–9
  religious, 48
religion. *See also* science and religion
  defined, 33
  dependent on the dialogue, 35
  diachronic understanding, 43
  erroneous understanding, 29
  faith contrasted, 96
  healthy and unhealthy, 58–59
  history of influence on science, 54
  internal factions, 136–37
  politicized, effect on the dialogue, 64
  questions revealed by science, 34–35
  rooted in culture, 57–59
  Science and Spiritual Quest, 65–67
  science compared, 53
  as a search for truth, 43–44
  spirituality compared, 96
  as systems of thought, 139
  tempering science, 3–4, 60
  transcending culture, 58
  universality vs. regionality, 47–48
religious relativism, 48
repeatability, 28, 42
respect, 125
Response Literature, 78–79
revelation, 69–70
Ṛgveda, 93
Ricci, Matteo, 122
right thinking and action (*dharma*), 92–93
Rolston, Holmes, III, vii, 33–37, 146
Rosen, Nathan, 107–09
Rosner, Fred, 80
Ruse, Michael, 122

the sacred, 34–35, 44
samādhi (trance), 98
sanctification, 128, 129
Schrödinger, Erwin, 112
science. *See also subsequent entries*
  à la Islam, 87–88
  Buddhism compared, 103, 107–09
  changing nature of, 35
  compelled by the Qur'an, 83–84
  defined, 33, 103
  emancipation needed, 56–57
  influence on religion in India, 95
  limits of, 16–20
  metaphysics compared, 7
  the metaquestion, 29–30
  modern, in India, 93–97
  realms beyond, 28
  religion compared, 53
  rooted in culture, 54–57
  as a search for truth, 43–44
  as self-limiting, 41–42
  and the spiritual quest, 65–67
  synchronic understanding, 42–43

technology contrasted, 27–28
tempering religion, 3, 53, 59, 60
as a threat, 9
topic for ecumenical dialogue, 49
universality vs. regionality, 47–48
valuing, 33–34
view of humanness, 47
as works of God, 75–76
yielding religious questions, 34–35
science and religion
after Indian independence, 95–97
the Asian Christian perspective, 121–33
the Buddhist perspective, 101–19
combined insights, 30–31
in a cultural context, 53–61
the Hindu perspective, 91–99
the Islamic perspective, 81–89
the Judaic perspective, 75–80
a natural synthesis, 29
past, present, and future, 41–51
science and religion dialogue
approaches, 59–60
background, vii
basic themes, 3–5
benefits, 22–24
bridge building metaphor, 122–23
Buddhist grounds, 101–04
core project, 3
in a cultural context, 53–61
cultural variety, 47
ecumenical nature, 49
explosion in the 1980s, 63
four challenges, 36
model: Science and Spiritual Quest, 65–69
model: the Asian trilogue, 125–28
motivations of the Abrahamic traditions, 69–70
recent evolution, 46–47
repairing recent damage, 64–65
two axes of motion, 135–36
a Western phenomenon, 121–22
why it matters, 27–32, 33–37
science and religion dialogue: topics
cloning, 142
complexity theory, 49–50
consciousness studies, 50–51
cosmology, 5–8
determinism, 11–16
emptiness, 129
ethics, 139–40
existence and the evidence of existence, 20–21
the limits of science, 16–20
the nature of humanity, 8–11, 11–16
the nature of the soul, 50
the nature of the universe, 5–8
neuroscience, 8–11, 50
organismic holism, 130–31
physics, 11–16
posthumanism, 143
species boundaries, 142–43
synthetic biology, 141
the tao of humanization, 129
technology, 139–41
theology of nature, 130, 138–39
time and causality, 129–30
views of reality, 48
Science and Spiritual Quest (SSQ), 65–69
Science and the Spiritual Quest in the Abrahamic Traditions (SSQAT), 68, 70
science of the mind, 103
scientific methodology
inapplicable to sacred texts, 87
intuition compared, 101
parallel in Buddhism, 103
potential of, 97
similarity to halakhic analysis, 76–77
Scientific Policy Resolution (India), 95
scientists and believers, 66

search for truth in science and religion, 43–44
the secular into the sacred, 34–35
secularization limited range of, 57
self-cultivation, 128, 129
selfish gene, 54
self-realization (*jñāna-mārga*), 92
self-restraint (*yama*), 97
self-so (*wu-wei*), 130
sense withdrawal (*pratyāhāra*), 98
Shulkhan Arukh, 78
Smith, Wilfred C., 122
social constructions, 13
sociobiology on the origin of ethics, 17
Soloveitchik, Joseph B., 76–77
soul, function of, 50
species boundaries, 142–43
spectacles analogy, 14–15
spiritual emancipation (*mokṣa*), 93
spiritual quest, 65–70
spirituality, 96, 128
SSQ. *See* Science and Spiritual Quest (SSQ)
SSQAT. *See* Science and the Spiritual Quest in the Abrahamic Traditions (SSQAT)
stem cells, 31
streams of consciousness, 116
string theory, 7–8
Subbarayappa, B. V., viii, 91–99, 147
substantialism, 129
subtle impermanence, 104
suffering, 35–36, 46
Susskind, L., 7
synchronic vs. diachronic understanding, 42–43
synchronicity, 130
synthetic biology, 141

T'ai-chi (Triune Great Universe), 131
Talmud, 78
tao of humanization, 127–29
Tawhid (unity of God), 81
technology
  contrasted with science, 27
  in the dialogue, 139–41
  tempered by wisdom, 31
temperance, 3–4
Templeton, John, 126
theanthropocosmic trajectory, 130–31
theism, to explain the nature of the universe, 6–7
theodicy, 129
theology of nature, 130, 138–39
Third World Academy of Sciences, viii, 61
"Thou" vs. "It," 28, 42
thought experiment, 103, 107–09
Thuan, Trinh Xuan, viii, 101–19, 147
time and causality, 129–30
top down causation, 12–13, 56
Tracy, David, 125
traditionalism across religions, 136–37
trance (*samādhi*), 98
transparency, rational, as evidence of a creator, 30
transpersonal realm, 28, 42
trilogue of humility, 125–28
Triune Great Universe (*T'ai-chi*), 131
truth
  absolute vs. relative, 60, 106, 115
  in the dialogue, 3–4
  of the Qur'an, 86
truth, search for
  Christianity and Judiasm compared, 57
  science and religion compared, 28–29, 43–44, 104

Unāni, 93
understanding, 27, 42–43
uniqueness, 42

unity, 81–83
unity of God (*Tawhid*), 81
universality in science and religion, 47–48
universe
  Buddhist view, 112–16
  inflationary era, 15
  nature of, 5–8, 112–14

vacuity, 110–12, 129
value-based living (*artha*), 92–93
values. *See also* ethics
  applied to science, 23
  in the dialogue, 4–5
  role in decisions, 18–19
  valuing nature and culture, 33–34
vertical vs. horizontal perspective, 47
volition, 12–13

Waldenburg, Eliezer, 79–80
war and peace, challenge of, 36
Waters, Brent, 143
Watts, Fraser, vii–viii, 53–61, 147
Western Christianity as a distortion, 121
wholistic perspective afforded by dialogue, 22–24
"why?" and "how?," 28, 29
Wigner, E. P., 44
Wilson, E. O., 34
written (Jewish) law, 78
wu-wei (self-so), 130

yama (self-restraint), 97
yoga, 97–99